THE LORD'S PRAYER

**TOUCHSTONE
TEXTS**

Stephen B. Chapman, Series Editor

THE LORD'S PRAYER

*Matthew 6 and Luke 11
for the Life of the Church*

WILLIAM M. WRIGHT IV

Baker Academic
a division of Baker Publishing Group
Grand Rapids, Michigan

© 2023 by William M. Wright IV

Published by Baker Academic
a division of Baker Publishing Group
Grand Rapids, Michigan
www.bakeracademic.com

Printed in the United States of America

Library of Congress Cataloging-in-Publication Data
Names: Wright, William M., IV, author.
Title: The Lord's prayer : Matthew 6 and Luke 11 for the life of the church / William M. Wright, IV.
Description: Grand Rapids, Michigan : Baker Academic, a division of Baker Publishing Group, [2023] | Series: Touchstone texts | Includes bibliographical references and index.
Identifiers: LCCN 2022033454 | ISBN 9781540963062 (cloth) | ISBN 9781493440269 (ebook) | ISBN 9781493440276 (pdf)
Subjects: LCSH: Lord's prayer—Criticism, interpretation, etc.
Classification: LCC BV230 .W755 2023 | DDC 226.9/606—dc23/eng/20220826
LC record available at https://lccn.loc.gov/2022033454

Unless otherwise indicated, quotations from the Dead Sea Scrolls are from Florentino García Martínez and Eibert J. C. Tigchelaar, eds. The Dead Sea Scrolls: Study Edition. 2 vols. Grand Rapids: Brill and Eerdmans, 2000.

Baker Publishing Group publications use paper produced from sustainable forestry practices and post-consumer waste whenever possible.

23 24 25 26 27 28 29   7 6 5 4 3 2 1

For my friends from Cleveland

"Faithful friends are a sturdy shelter:
whoever finds one has found a treasure.
Faithful friends are beyond price;
no amount can balance their worth."
—Sirach 6:14–15

"Among all worldly things, there is nothing which seems
preferable to proper friendship. . . . It is what brings the
greatest delights to such a degree that whatever delightful
things there are become tedious without friends; but love
makes tough things easy and as almost nothing."
—St. Thomas Aquinas, De regno ad regem Cypri I.11
(my translation)

Contents

Series Preface

In writing workshops, "touchstone texts" are high-quality writing samples chosen to illustrate teaching points about compositional techniques, genre conventions, and literary style. Touchstone texts are models that continually repay close analysis. The Christian church likewise possesses core scriptural texts to which it returns, again and again, for illumination and guidance.

In this series, leading biblical scholars explore a selection of biblical touchstone texts from both the Old Testament and the New Testament. Individual volumes feature theological exposition. To exposit a biblical text means to set forth the sense of the text in an insightful and compelling fashion while remaining sensitive to its interpretive challenges, potential misunderstandings, and practical difficulties. An expository approach interprets the biblical text as a word of God to the church and prioritizes its applicability for preaching, instruction, and the life of faith. It maintains a focus primarily on the biblical text in its received canonical form, rather than engaging in historical reconstruction as an end in itself (whether of the events behind the text or the text's literary formation). It listens to individual texts in concert with the rest of the biblical canon.

Each volume in this series seeks to articulate the plain sense of a well-known biblical text by what Aquinas called "attending to the way the words go" (*salva litterae circumstantia*). Careful exegesis is pursued either phrase by phrase or section by section (depending on the biblical text's length and genre). Authors discuss exegetical, theological, and pastoral concerns in combination rather than as discrete moves or units. They offer constructive interpretations that aim to transcend denominational boundaries. They consider the use of these biblical texts in current church practice (including the lectionary) as well as church history. The goal of the series is to model expositional interpretation and thereby equip Christian pastors and teachers to employ biblical texts knowledgeably and effectively within an ecclesial setting.

Texts were chosen for inclusion partly in consultation with the authors of the series. An effort was made to select texts that are representative of various biblical genres and address different facets of the Christian life (e.g., faith, blessing, morality, worship, prayer, mission, hope). These touchstone texts are all widely used in homiletics and catechesis. They are deserving of fresh expositions that enable them to speak anew to the contemporary church and its leaders.

Stephen B. Chapman
Series Editor

Acknowledgments

Most of the work on this project was done during the COVID-19 pandemic in 2020–21. There are many people whom I wish to thank for their help with this project, especially during that time. First of all, I thank my wife, Michelle, and my son, Will, for their support, encouragement, kindness, and love. I am so grateful for you and for our family.

I thank Stephen Chapman, the editor of the Touchstone Texts series, for his kind invitation to write this volume on the Lord's Prayer. Stephen also provided valuable editorial help that improved the final product. I also thank Nathan Eubank for reading through a draft of the entire manuscript and for his helpful comments and conversation. This project benefited much from their assistance, and all of its shortcomings are my own. Among others who have variously helped with this book, I think of Maggie and Charlie Garriott, my colleagues at Duquesne University, Bob McCambridge and the late Francis Martin, and Fr. Andrew Dalton, LC. I am also grateful to Jim Kinney, Bryan Dyer, Jennifer Koenes, and the team at Baker Academic. They do such excellent work with every part of the publication process.

It is with much gratitude that I dedicate this book to my close circle of friends from my hometown of Cleveland, Ohio. I have been friends with some of them from elementary school to high school, college, and beyond. Although I have had to move away from my hometown and despite our being an eclectic bunch, we share a bond of friendship that has not only endured but thrived for decades and through the many joys and tragedies of life. I count them among the greatest blessings in my life, and I would not be who I am today without them.

Abbreviations

Old Testament

Gen.	Genesis	Eccles.	Ecclesiastes
Exod.	Exodus	Song	Song of Songs
Lev.	Leviticus	Isa.	Isaiah
Num.	Numbers	Jer.	Jeremiah
Deut.	Deuteronomy	Lam.	Lamentations
Josh.	Joshua	Ezek.	Ezekiel
Judg.	Judges	Dan.	Daniel
Ruth	Ruth	Hosea	Hosea
1 Sam.	1 Samuel	Joel	Joel
2 Sam.	2 Samuel	Amos	Amos
1 Kings	1 Kings	Obad.	Obadiah
2 Kings	2 Kings	Jon.	Jonah
1 Chron.	1 Chronicles	Mic.	Micah
2 Chron.	2 Chronicles	Nah.	Nahum
Ezra	Ezra	Hab.	Habakkuk
Neh.	Nehemiah	Zeph.	Zephaniah
Esther	Esther	Hag.	Haggai
Job	Job	Zech.	Zechariah
Ps(s).	Psalm(s)	Mal.	Malachi
Prov.	Proverbs		

New Testament

Matt.	Matthew	John	John
Mark	Mark	Acts	Acts
Luke	Luke	Rom.	Romans

1 Cor.	1 Corinthians	Philem.	Philemon
2 Cor.	2 Corinthians	Heb.	Hebrews
Gal.	Galatians	James	James
Eph.	Ephesians	1 Pet.	1 Peter
Phil.	Philippians	2 Pet.	2 Peter
Col.	Colossians	1 John	1 John
1 Thess.	1 Thessalonians	2 John	2 John
2 Thess.	2 Thessalonians	3 John	3 John
1 Tim.	1 Timothy	Jude	Jude
2 Tim.	2 Timothy	Rev.	Revelation
Titus	Titus		

General

a.	answer	Hb.	Hebrew
alt.	altered, alternative	i.e.	id est, that is
ca.	circa, about, approximately	Lat.	Latin
		lit.	literally
chap(s).	chapter(s)	LXX	Septuagint
col.	column	no.	number
d.	died	par(r).	parallel(s)
frag.	fragment	q.	question
Gk.	Greek	v(v).	verse(s)

Bible Versions

KJV	King James Version	NRSV	New Revised Standard Version

Old Testament Apocrypha

Pr. Azar.	Prayer of Azariah	Tob.	Tobit
Sir.	Sirach (Ecclesiasticus)	Wis.	Wisdom (of Solomon)

Old Testament Pseudepigrapha

2 Bar.	2 Baruch (Syriac Apocalypse)	Jos. Asen.	Joseph and Aseneth
		Jub.	Jubilees
1 En.	1 Enoch	1–4 Macc.	1–4 Maccabees
4 Ezra	4 Ezra		

Qumran / Dead Sea Scrolls

1QH^a	Thanksgiving Hymns (Hodayot)	1QS	Rule of the Community (Serek Hayaḥad)

1QSa   Rule of the Congrega-
           tion (appendix a to 1QS)

Rabbinic Works and Tractates

Avot	Avot	Qidd.	Qiddushin
b.	Babylonian Talmud	Shabb.	Shabbat
Ber.	Berakhot	Ta'an.	Ta'anit
m.	Mishnah		

Apostolic Fathers

Did.   Didache

Other Early and Medieval Sources

Jerome, *Comm. Matt.*	*Commentary on Matthew*
Tertullian, *Or.*	*De oratione (Prayer)*
Thomas Aquinas, *De pot.*	*Quaestiones disputate de potentia Dei (On the Power of God)*

Bibliographic

BAGD   Bauer, Walter, William F. Arndt, F. Wilbur Gingrich, and Freder-
           ick W. Danker. *A Greek-English Lexicon of the New Testament
           and Other Early Christian Literature.* 2nd ed. Chicago: University
           of Chicago Press, 1979.

Introduction

During his earthly ministry, Jesus taught his disciples a prayer that has come to be known as the Our Father or the Lord's Prayer. Two versions of this prayer have been recorded in the New Testament, in Matthew 6:9–13 and Luke 11:2–4. From Christianity's beginnings to the present, Jesus's disciples have recited this prayer in public worship and in private piety.

In both Matthew and Luke, Jesus gives this prayer to his disciples as part of a larger set of teachings on prayer, but each Gospel locates these teachings in a different setting. While each Gospel has its own way of presenting the Lord's Prayer, both agree on the identity of the one who teaches it. As we begin our study, it is worth pausing to ask, What does it mean to call this prayer the *Lord's* Prayer?

In chapter 11 of his Gospel, Luke the Evangelist recounts an episode that begins with Jesus himself praying to the Father (11:1–4). After Jesus finishes his prayer, one of his disciples asks him, "Lord, teach us to pray, as John taught his disciples" (v. 1). Jesus agrees and goes on to teach his followers the Lord's Prayer (vv. 2–4). When this disciple makes this request, he addresses Jesus as "Lord" (*kyrie*). In Luke's Gospel, this Greek word, *kyrios*, has a range of meanings. It can be a term of respectful address like "sir," and it can also mean "master," such as when students respectfully address their teacher.[1] For Jesus's disciple to address him here as *kyrie* befits their teacher-student relation.

But when applied to Jesus in Luke's Gospel (and elsewhere), the title *kyrios* can not only indicate respectful address but also signify Jesus's divinity.[2] In the Greek edition of the Old Testament (i.e., the Septuagint or LXX), the word *kyrios* renders YHWH, the sacred name of the God of Israel. Luke follows this use of *kyrios* to designate the God of Israel, and when Luke calls Jesus *kyrios*, he includes Jesus in the identity of the God of Israel.[3] When Jesus teaches his disciples the Lord's Prayer, he gives them this prayer not simply as their teacher but as the Lord God himself.

A similar picture emerges from Matthew's Gospel. In Matthew, Jesus teaches the Lord's Prayer as part of the Sermon on the Mount (5:1–7:27). The Sermon on the Mount is the first of five great teaching discourses in Matthew's Gospel, and Jesus addresses this discourse to his disciples and the sympathetic crowds (4:25–5:2). The large amount of teaching material in Matthew's Gospel, along with its presentation of Jesus's teaching in five major discourses (to mirror the five books of the Law/Torah), highlights Matthew's concern to present Jesus as a teacher.

Similar to Luke, Matthew emphasizes that Jesus is not just another teacher: "He taught them as one having authority, and not as their scribes" (7:29).[4] Throughout Matthew's Gospel, many people recognize Jesus as a teacher and address him as such. However, the only ones in Matthew's Gospel who address Jesus with the titles "Teacher" or "Rabbi" are his opponents and those who do not believe in him.[5]

---

1. Examples of the use of *kyrios* along the lines of "sir" appear in Luke 7:6; 13:8; 14:22; 19:16. The use of *kyrios* as "master" in the context of a teacher-student relationship occurs in Luke 9:54, 61; 10:17, 40; 12:41.

2. See Rowe, *Early Narrative Christology*.

3. So Luke 1:6, 9, 16, 43; 2:11. This manner of framing things in terms of God's "identity" is indebted to the divine-identity Christology mapped out in Bauckham, *Jesus and the God of Israel*.

4. Following Holladay, *Critical Introduction*, 1:202, 204–5.

5. For such uses of "teacher," see Matt. 8:19; 9:11; 12:38; 22:16. For such uses of "rabbi," see Matt. 26:25, 49.

Whenever Jesus's disciples or others who are sympathetic to him address Jesus, they call him "Lord" (*kyrios*).[6] Anyone, even Jesus's opponents, can recognize that he is a teacher. But to think of Jesus only as a teacher is to misunderstand him and his teaching. The proper understanding of Jesus as a teacher entails that one recognize him in faith as the Lord, the Son of God (3:17), and Emmanuel—that is, "God . . . with us" (1:23).

Both Matthew and Luke thus present Jesus as a religious teacher when he is giving his disciples the Lord's Prayer. At the same time, both Matthew and Luke insist that Jesus is not merely a human teacher; he is the Lord himself. The Lord's Prayer, therefore, is a prayer that is taught to people by the Lord God.

The Lord's Prayer is an instance of divine teaching. By giving his disciples this prayer, the Lord is teaching us directly about who he is, about who we are, and about how we should relate to him and to each other. C. Clifton Black puts it well: "The Lord's Prayer explicates who we truly are: creatures made in God's image, warped by sin and under restoration by God's Holy Spirit. Simultaneously, the Prayer trains what we are becoming: God's obedient children, whose minds are renewed by God's merciful will."[7]

When we recite the Lord's Prayer, we approach the Father in prayer and with certain petitions. But we can do this only because the Father has first approached and taught us, through his Son, how we are to pray.[8] The Lord's Prayer comprises both our words to God and God's words to us.

The Approach Taken in This Book

In keeping with this series' stated concern of expositing touchstone texts of Scripture for the life of the church, this book approaches the Lord's Prayer as an eminent case of divine pedagogy that speaks to

---

6. Cf. Matt. 8:2, 6, 8, 25; 14:28, 30.
7. Black, *Lord's Prayer*, xxi.
8. I here anticipate the discussion of biblical prayer in chap. 1 and the valuable work of Seitz, "Prayer in the Old Testament," 3–22.

people in all places and times. As such, this study understands the Lord's Prayer in explicitly theological terms and with concern for how these scriptural words give us God's Word. It integrates exegetical analysis, theological exposition, and spiritual reflection with the goal of helping people come to know and love God and others more deeply. It is written from the perspective of creedal Christian faith and envisions its primary readership as sharing (or at least sympathizing with) this perspective.[9]

Our focus will be the so-called plain sense of the Lord's Prayer in the Gospels of Matthew and Luke. To use a common rendering of Thomas Aquinas's description, the plain sense of the biblical text pertains to "the way the words go [in context]."[10] For audiences today, the plain sense of the words can be illumined by our knowledge of the Gospels as historical, literary, and theological compositions of the first century. As we will discuss, the two versions of the Lord's Prayer given in the New Testament differ in some ways from each other—and there is a third version of the prayer in a late first-century Christian writing known as the Didache. Moreover, each biblical version of the Lord's Prayer fits within the larger literary and theological context of the Gospel in which it appears. Matthew and Luke are not simply transmitters but also interpreters of the Lord's Prayer. Each evangelist draws out dimensions of the prayer's meaning through the ways he gives the Greek wording of the prayer, locates it in his Gospel narrative, and connects it to other material in his Gospel. Attending to these matters can help us grasp dimensions of prayer that Matthew or Luke invites us to see. For as Thomas Aquinas affirms, the plain sense of Scripture can accommodate a variety of true interpretations.[11]

9. Accordingly, the text of this book will use first-person pronouns, such as "we" and "us."

10. The phrase "the way the words go" is the translation of Aquinas's phrase *salva circumstantia litterae* (*De pot.* q. 4, a. 1) given by Bruce D. Marshall in his "Absorbing the World," 93. I have added the bracketed phrase "in context" to bring out dimensions of Aquinas's larger argument in this passage about the context in which biblical words appear and also the sense of his Latin word *circumstantia* (i.e., what "stands" [*stantia*] "around" [*circum*] the words).

11. Aquinas writes, "One [should] not wish to force Scripture into one sense so as completely to exclude other senses that in themselves include truth and can accommodate Scripture in its context" (*De pot.* q. 4, a. 1). Aquinas, *Power of God*, 100.

Put negatively, this book is not an exercise in historical Jesus study, nor is it the kind of exegetical analysis that tries to determine the transmission history of the prayer, what reading of the prayer might be older than another, or how the prayer may have been given in Jesus's Aramaic speech. Such work has value, and we will at times make use of it. But our interests lie with the final form of the biblical text, for it is the final form that is ultimately inspired and normative for the church's life. That is to say, it is the final form that is Scripture.

The plain sense of the Lord's Prayer in the Gospels also needs to be taken in light of the larger context of the biblical canon—that is, its connections with other biblical texts. Jesus was a Jewish man of the first century. He thought and lived within the world of the Scriptures (i.e., the Old Testament or Hebrew Bible) and their expression in Jewish spirituality. We should not be surprised, therefore, that every line of the Lord's Prayer makes some degree of reference to the Old Testament. By so alluding to biblical texts and traditions, Jesus invites us to receive his words in light of the Scriptures. Furthermore, for their part, Matthew and Luke (like other New Testament authors) present Jesus as standing firmly within the Scriptures and history of Israel. The broader relationship between Jesus and the history of Israel given in the Gospels provides the setting for the Lord's Prayer. Interpreting the Lord's Prayer in light of the Old Testament is simply to follow the lead of both Jesus and the evangelists. They invite us to receive the Lord's Prayer in light of the Scriptures, and doing so is of great help in grasping the substance of the prayer.

We can also deepen our grasp of the Lord's Prayer by considering it in light of other New Testament writings. In this study, we aim to preserve the distinctive sense of the prayer as given in the Gospels of Matthew and Luke—and thus not have it absorbed or overpowered by other New Testament voices. To this end, we will place high priority on interpreting the Lord's Prayer within the Gospels of Matthew and Luke, respectively. At the same time, the Lord's Prayer has thematic and theological connections with other New Testament writings. For instance, there are two places in Paul's Letters (Rom. 8:15; Gal.

4:6) where he preserves the Aramaic word *'abbā'* ("father"), which was Jesus's distinctive term of address for God. Here Paul says that Christians, having been adopted by God the Father, can address and relate to him as Jesus does. Furthermore, Paul's Letters point us to the difference that Jesus's death and resurrection make for how Jesus's disciples relate to the Father. Jesus's death and resurrection enable a relationship with the Father that was not available to people beforehand. When Jesus's disciples say the Lord's Prayer after his resurrection, they say it in a different context than they could have before the resurrection. We will therefore incorporate into our exposition of the Lord's Prayer the theological contributions of related New Testament writings while prioritizing the distinctive voices of Matthew and Luke.

The Plan for This Book

Our study of the Lord's Prayer will feature seven chapters of unequal length. Chapter 1 places the Lord's Prayer in several relevant contexts. We begin with an initial examination of the two scriptural versions of the Lord's Prayer (Matt. 6:9–13; Luke 11:2–4) and place them within their respective Gospel contexts. We then expand our concern for context to the larger biblical canon. In particular, we situate the Lord's Prayer within the larger context of biblical prayer and reflect on biblical prayer as a form of divine pedagogy. Finally, we consider two matters of theological and religious context that are important for understanding the Lord's Prayer: the theological context of biblical eschatology and the religious setting of ancient Jewish spirituality and prayer.

Moving to the contents of the Lord's Prayer, chapter 2 is devoted entirely to Jesus's instructions to address God as "Father." We first situate this address within the biblical understanding of God as Father and the larger biblical view of the ideal relationship between a father and his son (or child).[12] The more proximate setting for ad-

---

12. As products of their ancient culture, the biblical writings frame things in terms of the relationship between fathers and sons. However, as we proceed in our

dressing God as Father, however, is Jesus's teaching about his own relationship with the Father, a relationship that he opens up to his disciples. We then draw these elements together and consider what it means for Christians to address God as Father in prayer.[13]

From here, we turn to the so-called "you" petitions of the Lord's Prayer: "hallowed be your name" (the name petition), "your kingdom come" (the kingdom petition), and "your will be done" (the will petition) (Matt. 6:9–10). These petitions are known as the "you" petitions because they all include the modifier "your" and specify something that is properly the Father's: *your* name, *your* kingdom, *your* will. Chapter 3 will treat the name petition, and chapter 4 will examine the kingdom and will petitions together, as they are thematically similar.

The other petitions of the Lord's Prayer are the "we" petitions, and these will be the focus of chapters 5, 6, and 7. Whereas the "you"

---

exposition, we will extend these insights to include daughters as well and thus speak of "children." The New Testament speaks of Christians, both men and women, as children of God (e.g., Rom. 8:16; 1 John 3:1–2). We will also signal cases where Jesus's obedience is connected to his identity as "Son" as well as texts that speak of Christians as God's adopted "sons" to show forth their participation in the reality of Jesus the "Son."

13. Throughout this book, I take the name "Father" to be the revealed, proper name of the First Person of the Trinity and will correspondingly use masculine pronouns for the deity (with the recognition that all perfections that appear in both males and females are present fully and undividedly in God). Several reasons can be briefly cited in this regard. First, in keeping with trinitarian orthodoxy, the name "Father" primarily designates a subsistent relation within the Trinity—not the Father's relation to any creature; that is, the Father is the Father because he is the father of the Son within the Godhead. Second, operating from a Thomistic perspective, I take the name "Father" to be a case of analogical (and not metaphorical) speech. Whereas (following W. Norris Clarke, cited below) metaphors are never literally true, analogical speech has some literal (albeit highly qualified) purchase on the reality of which it is predicated. While we cannot comprehend the nature of the Father's fatherhood, which itself differs profoundly from human fatherhood, there are some points of analogical similarity between these realities and predications that allow us to speak meaningfully about God. Third, the name "Father" is what Jesus, the incarnate Word and Son, has revealed to us. Given the radical transcendence and incomprehensibility of the Godhead, we can know God personally only insofar as God chooses to reveal himself. Jesus taught his disciples to use this name in relating to the one whom he called "Father." For discussion of the larger perspective adopted here, see Clarke, *One and the Many*, 42–59; DiNoia, "Knowing and Naming," 162–87; Emery, *Trinitarian Theology*, 151–75; White, *Trinity*, esp. 456–70.

petitions all include the modifier "your" and name something specific to the Father, the "we" petitions all ask the Father to do something for the disciples who pray: "Give *us* this day *our* daily bread" (the bread petition), "Forgive *us our* debts" (the forgiveness petition), and "Do not bring *us* to the time of trial" and "Rescue *us* from the evil one" (taken together here as the deliverance petition) (Matt. 6:11–13, emphasis added). Chapter 5 will treat the bread petition, and chapter 6 will cover the forgiveness petition. Chapter 7 will take up the petitions "Do not bring us to the time of trial" and "Rescue us from the evil one" (Matt. 6:13) and will treat them together as the deliverance petition.

Having completed our examination of the Lord's Prayer, we will draw together and synthesize the key points from the preceding chapters in a concluding summary.

1

The Lord's Prayer in Context

In a homily on the transfiguration, Saint Jerome states that we "inquire into the significance of the words in order to fathom the mystery contained in the text."[1] Following Jerome's insight, we begin our exposition of the theological substance of the Lord's Prayer with an initial examination of the language of the Lord's Prayer given in Matthew 6:9–13 and Luke 11:2–4. We will register similarities and differences between the two versions and consider what might account for them. This initial examination will set up the more focused attention to the language of each petition in the following chapters.

From here, we will place the Lord's Prayer in several relevant contexts that illumine the prayer's content and that can help us understand it better. First, we will consider the two versions of the Lord's Prayer in their respective literary contexts in the Gospels of Matthew and Luke. Second, we will expand our field of vision and place the Lord's Prayer within the larger context of the biblical canon. Specifically, we will consider the Lord's Prayer within the horizon of biblical prayer and reflect on biblical prayer as a form of divine pedagogy. Last,

---

1. Jerome, "Homily 80(VI)," in *Homilies of Saint Jerome*, 159. For a larger discussion of this statement in Jerome, see W. M. Wright, *Bible and Catholic Ressourcement*, 38–48.

we will discuss some relevant matters of theological and religious context. This includes a brief introduction to an area of biblical teaching called eschatology, and we will also examine some ancient Jewish prayers with which the Lord's Prayer has interesting similarities.

The Language of the Lord's Prayer: A First Look

The Two Versions of the Prayer

As mentioned above, there are two versions of the Lord's Prayer in the New Testament: Matthew 6:9–13 and Luke 11:2–4.[2] The two versions are similar in their structure and ideas and often in their wording. But there are also differences between these two versions of the prayer. At the outset, it is helpful to register the similarities and differences and begin to think about what difference the differences make.

Matthew 6:9–13

Content	English	Greek
Opening Address	Our Father in heaven,	*Pater hēmōn ho en tois ouranois,*
The "You" Petitions		
Name Petition	hallowed be your name.	*hagiasthētō to onoma sou.*
Kingdom Petition	Your kingdom come.	*Elthetō hē basileia sou.*
Will Petition	Your will be done, on earth as it is in heaven.	*Genēthētō to thelēma sou, hōs en ouranō kai epi gēs.*

2. The fact that the Lord's Prayer is shared between Matthew and Luke but does not appear in Mark leads most scholars to assign the Lord's Prayer to the hypothetical Q source. Some scholars have also argued that the two versions of the prayer represent independent lines of tradition. Moreover, there is a third version of the Lord's Prayer that comes to us in the Didache, a writing on church order that is roughly contemporary with the later writings of the New Testament. The version of the Lord's Prayer in Did. 8:2 (discussed below) likely depends on the version given in Matthew. For discussion of the tradition history of the Lord's Prayer, see Betz, *Sermon on the Mount*, 370–72; Black, *Lord's Prayer*, 45–48; Davies and Allison, *Gospel according to Saint Matthew*, 1:590–92; Luz, *Matthew 1–7*, 369–72.

Content	English	Greek
The "We" Petitions		
Bread Petition	Give us this day our daily bread.	*Ton arton hēmōn ton epiousion dos hēmin sēmeron.*
Forgiveness Petition	And forgive us our debts, as we also have forgiven our debtors.	*Kai aphes hēmin ta opheilēmata hēmōn, hōs kai hēmeis aphēkamen tois opheiletais hēmōn.*
Deliverance Petitions	And do not bring us to the time of trial, but rescue us from the evil one.	*Kai mē eisenenkēs hēmas eis peirasmon, alla rhysai hēmas apo tou ponērou.*

Luke 11:2–4

Content	English	Greek
Opening Address	Father,	*Pater,*
The "You" Petitions		
Name Petition	hallowed be your name.	*hagiasthētō to onoma sou.*
Kingdom Petition	Your kingdom come.	*Elthetō hē basileia sou.*
The "We" Petitions		
Bread Petition	Give us each day our daily bread.	*Ton arton hēmōn ton epiousion didou hēmin to kath' hēmeran.*
Forgiveness Petition	And forgive us our sins, for we ourselves forgive everyone indebted to us.	*Kai aphes hēmin tas hamartias hēmōn, kai gar autoi aphiomen panti opheilonti hēmin.*
Deliverance Petition	And do not bring us to the time of trial.	*Kai mē eisenenkēs hēmas eis peirasmon.*

Both versions of the Lord's Prayer have the same basic structure. First, there is the opening address in which we call on the Father by name. After the opening address, there are several petitions known as the "you" petitions. They are called the "you" petitions because they all center on something proper to the Father and contain the adjective "your." In these petitions, we speak to the Father of "*your* name," "*your* kingdom," and "*your* will" (Matt. 6:9–10, emphasis added). The next petitions are called the "we" petitions. They are called the "we" petitions because they center on something pertaining to humans and feature the words "us" and "our." Here we ask the Father to provide "*us*" with "*our*" bread, to "forgive *us our* sins" as "*we*" forgive those who sin against "*us*" (Luke 11:3–4, emphasis added), and not to lead "*us* to the time of trial" and to "rescue *us* from the evil one" (Matt. 6:11–13, emphasis added).

There are also some differences in content between the two versions of the prayer. Luke begins with the simple address "Father." But Matthew's version of the opening address includes two modifiers: Matthew speaks of him as "our Father" and as being "in heaven." Matthew's version also has two petitions that are not in Luke: "Your will be done, on earth as it is in heaven" and "Rescue us from the evil one."

The wording of the petitions in Matthew and Luke exhibits both similarities and differences. On the one hand, there are some places where Matthew and Luke give the exact same Greek wording of a petition. This occurs in the name, kingdom, and (the first part of) the deliverance petitions. But there are places where, although the ideas are similar, Matthew and Luke word a petition differently. For instance, in the bread petition, Matthew reads "this day," but Luke has "each day." In the forgiveness petition, Matthew's version speaks of "debts" and "our debtors." But Luke's version has "sins" and "everyone indebted to us." Matthew and Luke also have different readings after the forgiveness petition: Matthew has "as we also have forgiven our debtors" (6:12); Luke has "for we ourselves forgive everyone indebted to us" (11:4).

There are also more subtle differences in the Greek syntax of some petitions, and these subtleties give each version of the Lord's Prayer a somewhat different tone. This topic requires some discussion of the mechanics of ancient Greek. In Matthew's version, all the verbs (with one exception) are imperatives, and they are in the aorist tense. The aorist tense usually articulates a particular, simple action that has been completed (e.g., "I said" or "I wrote"). When an imperative appears in the aorist tense (as they do in Matthew's prayer), it generally expects an action to be completed on a single occasion.[3] But it is hard to tell just how much interpretive significance to see in this subtlety of syntax. If taken as maximally significant, the aorist verbs in Matthew's version would give the expectation of the Father granting these petitions on a particular occasion in the future. The future occasion to which these petitions would be looking is Jesus's parousia, the manifestation of the glorified Jesus as Lord and Judge at the end of days when he will bring the divine plan to its full realization (i.e., what is more popularly known as the second coming of Christ).

Luke's version of the Lord's Prayer also has a future orientation and contains some aorist imperatives. But Luke's version also features some present tense verbs, which temper a future orientation. For instance, in the bread petition, Luke's articulation of the verb "give" (*didou*) is a present imperative. Whereas an aorist imperative can look for an action to be completed on one occasion, a present tense imperative looks for an action to be repeated on many occasions or to keep going on.[4] In this way, Luke's version of the bread petition asks the Father to provide sustenance to his children continually. This sense of the Father's continual or ongoing action is supported by Luke's use of the adverbial phrase "each day" (i.e., provide us with sustenance every day). So like Matthew's, Luke's version of the Lord's Prayer has a future-looking tone as well, but his use of present tense

---

3. See Blass, Debrunner, and Funk, *Greek Grammar*, §335 (p. 172); Béchard, *Syntax of New Testament Greek*, §3.1 (pp. 37–39).
4. See Blass, Debrunner, and Funk, *Greek Grammar*, §335 (p. 172); Béchard, *Syntax of New Testament Greek*, §3.1 (pp. 37–39).

verbs amplifies the "life in the meanwhile" (the time before Jesus's parousia) a bit more than Matthew's version does.

Interpretive Adaptation

Several decades elapsed from when Jesus taught his disciples this prayer to when the evangelists recorded their two versions in the Gospels. During this time, the Lord's Prayer underwent some interpretive adaptations as it was translated and used in Christian practice. Consider, for instance, the basic matter of language and idiom. When Jesus taught this prayer to his disciples, he most likely taught it to them in Aramaic, the common language in the land of Israel in Jesus's day. But the versions of the prayer in Matthew and Luke are in Greek. And so, at a very basic level, the Lord's Prayer required translation from Aramaic to Greek (and then from Greek into the many other languages in which it has since come to people).

Some of the differences in wording illustrate the dynamics of interpretive adaptation. For instance, Matthew's version of the forgiveness petition reads, "Forgive us our debts" (6:12), and Luke's version has "Forgive us our sins" (11:4). In Jesus's day, the Aramaic word for "debt" (ḥōb) was a common idiom for sin. It was part of a larger trend in Jewish antiquity to talk about sin, forgiveness, atonement, and good works with economic language (e.g., debt, credit, remission).[5] It is therefore quite likely that Jesus would have used the word "debt" when teaching this prayer in Aramaic. Both Matthew and Luke preserve the debt language in the follow-up clause of the forgiveness petition. But before mentioning our forgiving "everyone indebted to us," Luke first gives the expression "Forgive us our sins" (11:4). In this way, Luke interprets the figurative meaning of "debt" for those in his audience who would not know the Aramaic idiom. The same idea is given in both versions of the prayer, but Luke has adapted the language so his audience would be able to understand its meaning.

---

5. See G. Anderson, *Sin*, esp. 27–39; Eubank, *Wages of Cross-Bearing*, 25–52.

Other examples of interpretive adaptation may be those petitions in Matthew's version of the Lord's Prayer that are not present in Luke's: the will petition and the petition for deliverance from the evil one. Now, it is possible that Jesus taught this prayer to his disciples on more than one occasion and with minor adjustments. It is also possible that with certain details and contents unique to his version of the prayer, Matthew could be providing what could be thought of as an interpretive elaboration of Jesus's words.[6] For instance, Matthew includes two mentions of "heaven" in his version of the prayer. As Jonathan Pennington has shown, the mentions of "heaven" in the Lord's Prayer square with a larger thematic concern in Matthew to contrast heaven and earth as separate realms that will be integrated at the end of days.[7] Moreover, those petitions that are only in Matthew— the will petition and the second part of the deliverance petition—can be thought of as drawing out the meaning of the preceding line. Thus, the petition "Your will be done, on earth as it is in heaven" expands the preceding petition "Your kingdom come" (Matt. 6:10). In other words, it is when the Father brings his kingdom to earth that his will is going to be done on earth as it is in heaven. Similarly, the petition "Rescue us from the evil one" clarifies by expansion the meaning of "Do not bring us to the time of trial" (6:13). In both cases, we ask the Father to keep us faithful to him when we are besieged by the powers of evil. And so, irrespective of whether these uniquely Matthean petitions stem from Jesus or whether they represent the early church's explication and liturgical use of the Lord's Prayer, they shed light on the substance of other petitions to which they are thematically related.

Matthew and Luke give us this prayer in such a way that each evangelist draws out different aspects of its meaning. A helpful analogy for understanding these dynamics comes from Raymond Brown. He uses the example of examining a precious stone that is on public display and appreciating its different sides and dimensions: "The diamond is on a stand in the center encased in glass, lighted from all sides;

6. So too Black, *Lord's Prayer*, 47–48.
7. Pennington, *Heaven and Earth*, 150–55.

when one enters one can see one side of it and admire the beauty, but it is only by walking around all four sides that one sees the whole of the stone and all the beauty. The variations that the evangelists have preserved, or even have themselves promoted, are differing insights into the same teaching of Jesus."[8] To apply Brown's analogy to this project, the Lord's Prayer is the precious stone on display. As the same stone is given to viewers who look at it from different sides and angles, so the prayer of Jesus is given to us from different "sides" in Matthew and Luke. Each presentation of the prayer draws out dimensions of its significance. By presenting the prayer as they do, the evangelists help us to hear and understand Jesus and, through him, to come to know and relate to the Father.

Excursus: The Lord's Prayer in the Didache

There is another version of the Lord's Prayer that appears in an ancient Christian writing known as the Didache ("the Teaching"). The Didache is a manual for church life and discipline that is usually dated to the late first or early second century. In a number of places, the Didache resonates strongly with the Gospel according to Matthew. It is very likely that the author and audience of the Didache knew Matthew, and the Didache probably emerged in the same locale in first-century Christianity as Matthew (often identified as Antioch in northern Syria). While we will not discuss the version of the Lord's Prayer given in the Didache, it is worth noticing that its wording closely aligns with that of Matthew. Also, a version of the doxology with which many Christians close the Lord's Prayer appears in the Didache but not in our oldest manuscripts of Matthew's Gospel.

8. Brown, *Responses to 101 Questions*, 64. Though he does not say so, what Brown proposes here is quite similar to the philosophical notion of identity in manifolds, which is a key component in phenomenology. It is the idea that a thing is given to a variety of knowing subjects in a manifold of appearances, without being reduced to any single appearance. On this matter, see Sokolowski, *Introduction to Phenomenology*, 17–21, 27–33. For an application of this phenomenological idea to biblical interpretation, see Wright and Martin, *Encountering the Living God*, 183–87, 214–15.

Didache 8:2

English	Greek
Our Father in heaven,	*Pater hēmōn ho en tō ouranō,*
hallowed be your name,	*hagiasthētō to onoma sou,*
your kingdom come,	*elthetō hē basileia sou,*
your will be done on earth as it is in heaven.	*genēthētō to thelēma sou hōs en ouranō kai epi gēs.*
Give us today our daily bread,	*Ton arton hēmōn ton epiousion dos hēmin sēmeron,*
and forgive us our debt, as we also forgive our debtors;	*kai aphes hēmin tēn opheilēn hēmōn, hōs kai hēmeis aphiemen tois opheiletais hēmōn;*
and do not lead us into temptation,	*kai mē eisenenkēs hēmas eis peirasmon,*
but deliver us from the evil one;	*alla rhysai hēmas apo tou ponērou;*
for yours is the power and the glory forever.	*hoti sou estin hē dynamis kai hē doxa eis tous aiōnas.*

* Text and translation in Holmes, *Apostolic Fathers*, 356–57.

The Lord's Prayer in the Context of the Gospels

The Lord's Prayer in Matthew

Matthew's version of the Lord's Prayer appears in the Sermon on the Mount (5:1–7:27). Taken as a whole, the Sermon on the Mount presents Jesus's messianic teaching on "righteousness" with regard to the kingdom. A core scriptural topic, righteousness (Hb. *ṣədāqâ*; Gk. *dikaiosynē*), as concerns human beings, designates the uprightness of life that is pleasing to God and rightly related to him.

The Lord's Prayer is embedded within a section of the sermon that treats three acts of righteous living: almsgiving, prayer, and fasting

(Matt. 6:1–18). These practices are all staple elements in Jewish piety.[9] The treatment of each practice here exhibits a similar pattern. First, Jesus introduces the practice. Next he gives a negative example of how not to perform it. Then Jesus provides positive instruction on how his disciples should live out these practices.

A common theme in Jesus's teaching about these spiritual practices is the need to have the right goal in performing them. In particular, Jesus warns against performing these actions for the sake of winning attention and admiration from others. Jesus's disciples are not to give alms "so that they may be praised by others" (Matt. 6:2), or pray "that they may be seen by others" (6:5), or fast with a "dismal" appearance "so as to show others that they are fasting" (6:16). Performing these actions for the purpose of enhancing one's reputation is wrongheaded and not pleasing to the Father. The "reward" paid out by these actions comes not from the Father but takes the form of the attention that one seeks and receives from others by such displays (6:2, 5, 16).[10]

When Jesus turns to the positive instructions, he again emphasizes the need to perform these actions for the right reason. He does so by repeatedly speaking of the need to perform them "in secret" (Matt. 6:4, 6, 18). "Secrecy" describes the correct way to perform these actions because it is the very opposite of self-serving, attention-seeking performance. To perform these actions "in secret" is to perform them primarily with God in mind and not the praise one might receive from others. Thus, instead of giving alms, praying, or fasting for the purpose of winning honor and attention from other people, Jesus instructs his disciples to do these things for God, "and your Father who sees in secret will reward you" (6:4, 6, 18).

In his instructions on prayer, Jesus cites two examples of what not to do. Jesus begins the section on prayer with an example from Jewish prayer practices: "Whenever you pray, do not be like the hypocrites;

9. Cf. Neh. 1:4; Ps. 35:13; Dan. 9:3; Tob. 4:7–10; 12:8–9; 14:8–11; Sir. 29:8, 12; Luke 2:37; 5:33; Acts 10:2, 4; 13:3; 14:23.
10. Helpful here is Eubank, *Wages of Cross-Bearing*, 78–80.

for they love to stand and pray in the synagogues and at the street corners" (Matt. 6:5). As we will discuss below, an important ancient Jewish prayer is the Amidah, and the one praying would recite it while standing.[11] But the issue here is not one's posture but one's purpose. Jesus disapproves when prayers are said "so that they may be seen by others" (6:5).[12] By contrast, Jesus uses a threefold description of praying differently: "Go into your room and shut the door and pray to your Father who is in secret" (6:6). Instead of praying for the purpose of attracting honor from others, Jesus tells his disciples to pray to the Father "who is in secret; and your Father who sees in secret will reward you" (6:6).

Jesus then provides a second negative example, drawn from gentile praying practices. He says, "Do not heap up empty phrases as the Gentiles do; for they think that they will be heard because of their many words" (Matt. 6:7). David Aune observes that it was customary in prayer formulas from the Greco-Roman world to address a particular deity with a long series of titles. He writes, "Not only must a divinity be addressed with precision and courtesy, but such invocation must also be accompanied by the formal titles, powers, and attributes of the deity if he or she is to hear the prayer."[13] It is arguably to this practice that Jesus refers when he speaks of "heap[ing] up empty phrases."

Jesus highlights the deeper presupposition that this gentile practice of prayer implies: listing honorary titles or hitting on the correct

11. The name Amidah is related to the Hebrew verb ʿāmad, which means "stand."
12. Referencing m. Taʾan. 4, Joachim Jeremias states that groups of Jews (known as "standing posts" [maʿamadot]), who were attached to specific rotations of priests on duty at the temple, would offer prayers both at the temple and wherever they would be in public to accompany the three hours of the day when sacrifices were offered at the temple (morning, afternoon at three o'clock, and sunset). This practice may very well stand behind Jesus's decrying those who "love to stand and pray in the synagogues and at the street corners, so that they may be seen" (Matt. 6:5). See Jeremias, *Prayers of Jesus*, 70–75. Similarly, the Didache says that the Lord's Prayer should be recited by Christians three times a day (Did. 8:3), a practice that would dovetail with the Jewish practice of praying three times a day (cf. Jeremias, *Prayers of Jesus*, 69–72, 78–81).
13. Aune, "Prayer in the Greco-Roman World," 36.

name is what attracts a deity's attention and hopefully gains a favorable response from him or her. By contrast, Jesus teaches that his disciples should not approach the Father in this way, because the Father is not like any pagan deity. The Father does not need to learn of one's needs, because "your Father knows what you need before you ask him" (Matt. 6:8). The Father does not need to be addressed with a long string of epithets and honorifics in order for one to gain his favor. Rather, the disciples are to approach and address God as their Father who loves them and knows them intimately. It is after this second negative example taken from gentile prayer practices that Jesus teaches his disciples the Lord's Prayer as the positive example of how they are to pray.

The Sermon on the Mount has been composed so that Jesus's teaching about these three practices—almsgiving, prayer, and fasting (Matt. 6:1–18)—lies at its very center.[14] Within this section on spiritual practices, the teachings on prayer (6:5–15) occupy the central position, for they are bracketed by the teachings on almsgiving (6:1–4) and fasting (6:16–18). The Lord's Prayer, therefore, sits at the very center point of the entire Sermon on the Mount. By so arranging the Sermon on the Mount, which is devoted to Jesus's teaching on righteous living, Matthew invites us to see the Lord's Prayer at the center of Jesus's teaching on righteousness—and thus the whole Christian life.

At a basic level, the centrality of the Lord's Prayer in the Sermon on the Mount speaks to the fundamental importance of prayer in the Christian life. Prayer is a form of personal communication. As communication is essential to forming and maintaining relationships between people, so too is prayer (analogously) essential to the personal relationship of human beings with God. Prayer is important not because God requires our prayers but because *we need* to approach and relate to God in this way. In prayer, we present to God ourselves and our various concerns (e.g., our thanks, praise, needs, repentance, etc.). And in prayer, we open ourselves to God and his activity within us. Prayer is fundamentally important to the life of

---

14. See Davies and Allison, *Gospel according to Saint Matthew*, 1:63–64.

righteousness because it is fundamentally important to a personal relationship with a personal God.

At a deeper level, the Lord's Prayer concerns our relationship with the Father specifically. Later in Matthew, Jesus explicitly declares that as the Son he alone can reveal the Father (11:27). With this prayer, Jesus teaches us about the Father and the distinctive relationship with the Father that he alone makes possible for his disciples. Jesus also invites his disciples to approach God and relate to him as our loving Father. This is the essence of the Christian life and Christian prayer: our relationship with the Father, through his Son Jesus, animated by the Holy Spirit. By growing in our relationship with the Father, we come to know more deeply his goodness and generous love: "If you then, who are evil, know how to give good gifts to your children, how much more will your Father in heaven give good things to those who ask him" (7:11).

The Lord's Prayer in Luke

Luke's Gospel has an abbreviated version of what Matthew presents as the Sermon on the Mount: the so-called Sermon on the Plain (Luke 6:17–49). But Luke does not locate the Lord's Prayer here. Instead, Luke presents the Lord's Prayer in an episode in the journey narrative (9:51–19:27). In this section of Luke's Gospel, Jesus travels from Galilee to Jerusalem with the Twelve and some other disciples in order to celebrate Passover. It is at this Passover that Jesus will bring about "his exodus" (9:31, my translation) and "finish [his] work" (13:32). Spanning nearly ten chapters of Luke's Gospel, the journey narrative features a concentration of Jesus's teachings.

The Lord's Prayer appears in a section where Jesus teaches his disciples about prayer (Luke 11:1–13). This section on prayer is framed by references to the Father at the very beginning and end (11:2, 13), and it has three component parts. First, Jesus teaches the Lord's Prayer in response to a disciple's request (11:1–4). Second, Jesus tells the parable of the persistent neighbor, a parable unique to Luke's Gospel that speaks to the need to be persistent in asking God for help (11:5–8). Third, in words that also appear in the Sermon on the Mount (11:9–13; cf. Matt. 7:7–11), Jesus encourages his disciples to "Ask . . . search . . . [and] knock," and the Father, who is good and loving, will give "the Holy Spirit to those who ask him" (Luke 11:9, 13).

Luke introduces these teachings on prayer by showing Jesus himself praying (11:1). While all the Gospels present Jesus praying to the Father, Luke does so in a deliberate and extensive way. Throughout his narrative, Luke distinctively presents Jesus praying at significant moments in his public ministry: after his baptism (3:21), before he chooses the twelve apostles (6:12), before he asks them "Who do the crowds say that I am?" (9:18), before and during the transfiguration (9:28–29), and when he teaches the Lord's Prayer (11:1–4). With Matthew and Mark, Luke depicts Jesus praying at length in Gethsemane before his arrest (22:41, 44–46), and Luke also has Jesus praying while on the cross (23:34, 45). Not only does Jesus instruct his disciples to pray (and gives them a prayer to recite), but he himself also prays to the Father, giving his followers an example to imitate. In this way, Luke follows the conventional practice in ancient ethical teaching of providing examples for people to imitate.[15]

Other elements in Luke's presentation of the Lord's Prayer fit with the motif of Jesus as a teacher. The teaching of the Lord's Prayer is occasioned by a disciple who asks Jesus on behalf of the group, "Teach us to pray, as John taught his disciples" (Luke 11:1). It was customary for religious teachers to prescribe forms of piety for their disciples to practice (cf. 5:33). When the disciple asks Jesus to teach their group to pray, he compares Jesus and John the Baptist: both are religious teachers who have a group of followers. As John the Baptist has taught his followers how to pray, this disciple looks for Jesus, as the group's religious teacher, to do the same.

After teaching his disciples the Lord's Prayer (Luke 11:2–4), Jesus continues with further instruction on this topic. He tells the parable of the persistent neighbor (11:5–8) and adds the "Ask, and it will be given you" sayings (11:9–13). Three elements connect this material

15. Malherbe, *Moral Exhortation*, 135–38.

with the Lord's Prayer. First, these blocks of teaching on prayer all involve different interpersonal relationships. The parable depicts a relationship between two friends (and neighbors), and in the "Ask, and it will be given you" section, the relationship is that of a father and his son. These examples square with the Lord's Prayer, in which the relationship is between Jesus's disciples and the Father. These examples underscore the interpersonal and relational nature of prayer.

Second, in the material after the Lord's Prayer, Jesus emphasizes the need to pray frequently and persistently. In the parable, a person goes to his friend for help in the middle of the night, asking for food to show hospitality to a guest who has just arrived. In a surprising response, the annoyed and awakened neighbor refuses to help his friend in need (Luke 11:7). Jesus closes the parable by remarking that even if the awakened man should refuse to help despite their friendship, he will end up helping if only to get his needy friend to stop bothering him (11:8). The awakened man's response is neither friendly nor altruistic. But it illustrates that persistence in asking can bring positive results even in imperfect human relationships. After this, Jesus further encourages his disciples to be persistent in prayer by phrasing the matter in terms of three activities: "Ask . . . search . . . knock" (11:9). He says that those who do so will obtain the goal of these activities: "Everyone who asks receives, and everyone who searches finds, and for everyone who knocks, the door will be opened" (11:10). Prayer, therefore, should be a continuous and persistent activity of Jesus's followers and a regular part of the disciples' lives.

In Luke 11:1–13, Jesus teaches that the Father wants us to speak and interact with him and to do so continually. Unlike the awakened man in the parable, the Father wants us to speak with him constantly and to "ask . . . search . . . [and] knock." While we may get annoyed with others when they speak to us incessantly or at an inopportune time, it is not so with the Father. One might say that the Father wants our constant attention and wants us to bother him all the time with our prayers—and he will never become annoyed with us or tired of our talking to him.

Third, Jesus also clarifies the nature of petitioning the Father and his answering our prayers. When Jesus teaches "Everyone who asks receives" (Luke 11:10), one might think him to mean that the Father will grant any request made of him. However, the example of fathers and sons provides important direction on this matter (11:11–12). In the examples, no (decent) human father would give something harmful (e.g., a snake or scorpion) to his son when his son asks him for food. Jesus then moves from this lesser case of human fathers to the greater case of the heavenly Father. He reasons that if human fathers, who are themselves sinful and flawed, "know how to give good gifts," how much more of a good, generous giver is the heavenly Father (11:13).

The gift of the Father that Jesus singles out is "the Holy Spirit" (Luke 11:13). As the risen Jesus says to the disciples on Easter Sunday evening, the Holy Spirit is "the promise of the Father" (24:49, my translation; Acts 1:4). The Holy Spirit who will come to indwell Jesus's disciples is the gift of God's own life within them. The indwelling of the Holy Spirit is the new covenant, announced by Ezekiel and made available to people through Jesus's Paschal Mystery (Ezek. 36:24–28).[16] As the gift of God, who incorporates human beings into the divine life of the Son and thus into a filial relationship with the Father, the Holy Spirit is the most precious of gifts indeed.

The Lord's Prayer in the Context of Biblical Prayer and Pedagogy

Biblical Prayer

Christopher Seitz makes the following statement about prayer, broadly understood, in the Old Testament: "Prayer turns on an in-

---

16. Although the phrase "new covenant" does not appear in Ezek. 36:24–28, this section contains a number of elements speaking to a renewal of the covenant attending God's end-time act of restoration, including the covenant formula "You shall be my people, and I will be your God" (Ezek. 36:28). Animating the new covenant relationship is the Spirit of God, whom God will put inside his redeemed people: "I will put my spirit within you, and make you follow my statutes" (36:27). For discussion, see Zimmerli, *Ezekiel 2*, 249. Thomas Aquinas (*Summa Theologiae* I-II, q. 106, a. 1) similarly speaks of the grace of the indwelling Holy Spirit as the new covenant.

timate knowledge of the named God of Israel, who revealed who he is to a particular people at the Red Sea and at Mt. Sinai—and who, on these terms and this ground, is accessible in prayer. Prayer in the Old Testament . . . is to talk with the living God! And to talk with the living God is, for Israel, to know God's name."[17] There are several points in this statement to highlight. First, at a basic level, prayer is speaking with God. It is an act of communication. When we pray, we communicate to God our praise, our thanks, our requests, our sufferings and complaints. We do so with the awareness that not only is God accessible to us, but he hears our prayers: our words, thoughts, and gestures can reach God, who knows them all.

Second, Seitz points out that prayer involves "an intimate knowledge" of God, who has "revealed" himself to the people Israel. This observation helps us to realize that our prayer to God does not really begin with us. Instead, our prayer actually begins with God. In order for us to have any personal knowledge of the radically transcendent God of the Bible (and thus communicate with him), God takes the first step and makes himself known to us. God does this by revealing himself in both word and action over the course of the divine economy. We are able to speak with God because God has spoken to us first. As Seitz writes, prayer "is the consequence of [God's] having made himself known and our faithful response to that prior knowledge."[18]

These first two points converge in a third: prayer is an interpersonal activity. Seitz speaks of the importance of God's name for the practice of prayer: "To talk with the living God is, for Israel, to know God's name." A person's name in the biblical tradition was an articulation of that person's identity and role in the world. While the God of Israel is not "a thing," he is personal, and in the Old Testament, God reveals his personal self in a special way when he reveals his name to Moses on Mount Sinai (Exod. 3:14). This is the name YHWH, usually translated into English as "LORD."

17. Seitz, "Prayer in the Old Testament," 5–6.
18. Seitz, "Prayer in the Old Testament," 15.

God is personal and has made himself known to us in the economy of salvation. In prayer, we, as human persons, communicate ourselves and our concerns to the God who has first revealed himself to us. The interpersonal dimension of prayer in the biblical tradition appears, as Seitz points out, in the practice of addressing God by name in prayer.[19] The psalms routinely feature the invocation "O LORD" when speaking to the God of Israel. And as Seitz argues, this role of God's name in biblical prayer reminds us that we can address God by name in prayer only because he has first revealed himself (i.e., his name) to us. Our prayer depends on and is a response to God's gracious self-revelation.

Our ability to pray to God is itself a gift from God. Not only does the radically transcendent God take the initiative and make himself known to us (i.e., he speaks to us), but God also invites us to respond to him in prayer. When we pray, we are personally interacting with the Creator and Lord of the entire universe, who has given us access to him at every moment of every day. All of this is a free, undeserved gift to us from God, given out of love. God does all of this because he *wants us* to respond to him in prayer.

But not only does God want us to talk with him; he has also given us some words to use when we do speak to him. These words come to us in the prayers within the Bible itself; the Lord's Prayer is one such prayer. Thinking more deeply about the character of scriptural prayers and how these prayers function when they are read as part of the Bible will give us further insight into the Lord's Prayer as an instance of divine pedagogy.

Biblical Prayers and Divine Pedagogy

The Scriptures contain many literary genres and modes of discourse. Among the catalog of literary genres, a variety of prayers

19. At the same time, the reverential recognition of the holiness of God and the holiness of his name informs the Jewish practice of never pronouncing his sacred name "YHWH." Instead, Jewish tradition uses a substitute word in such address, such as the Hebrew word *'ădōnāy* ("my Lord") or *haššēm* ("the Name").

and hymns appear in both the Old and the New Testaments. Most prominently, there is the collection of 150 prayers and hymns from ancient Israel known as the book of Psalms. Embedded within the narratives of the Old Testament, there are, for example, the hymn of praise following the Lord's deliverance of the Israelites at the Red Sea (Exod. 15:1–21), the Song of Moses (Deut. 32:1–43; cf. 31:19–22), the Song of Deborah (Judg. 5:2–31), and the prayer of Solomon at the dedication of the Jerusalem temple (1 Kings 8:22–61). Within the New Testament, one thinks of the songs of heavenly worship found in the book of Revelation and texts in Paul's Letters that might be parts of early Christian prayers or hymns (e.g., 1 Cor. 8:6; Phil. 2:6–11; Col. 1:15–20). And, of course, there is the Lord's Prayer in Matthew and Luke.

Biblical prayers are curious things. These prayers are human words directed to God. They were composed by human beings who themselves belonged to faith communities (i.e., the people Israel and the church) and were used (and continue to be used) in public worship and individual devotion. These prayers articulate verbally the spirituality of their authors, who are themselves part of a larger covenant community. At the same time, these human prayers, having been inspired by the Holy Spirit and canonized as part of Scripture, also mediate God's Word to us. When these prayers came to be incorporated into the biblical canon, they came to be recognized in faith as communicating God's Word.[20] So when we recite these biblical prayers in faith, not only are we speaking to God, but God is also speaking to us.

As an example of these dynamics, consider the book of Psalms. Scholars have recognized that within the Psalter there are different kinds or genres of psalms (e.g., laments, prayers of thanksgiving, hymns of praise, etc.). The psalms moreover exhibit a variety of poetic and rhetorical features, and many psalms, it seems, were set to music. Individual psalms were composed at particular moments in the history

---

20. For a theological analysis of these matters, see Farkasfalvy, *Theology of the Christian Bible*, esp. 159–98.

of Israel, and many came to be associated in various ways with the worship of God at the Jerusalem temple. These prayers were part of the spiritual life of God's people from when they were first composed, used, and collected.[21] Eventually these collections of prayers were assembled into the larger, organized collection of 150 that we call the book of Psalms.

Once canonized as Scripture, the psalms became part of the spiritual life of Jews and Christians in a new way: not only are they prayers, but they are also Scripture. Within the faith community, the Scriptures are received as mediating divine teaching, and thus they serve as an instrument by which God forms the thinking and living of his people. When texts like the psalms are taken as part of the larger scope of the biblical canon, they come to be seen as a part of a larger pedagogy by which God teaches and forms his people. As Robert Sokolowski writes, the psalms "articulate the various human sentiments and thoughts we should have in response to the understanding of God that was being revealed when they were written."[22] In these scriptural prayers, God is revealing something both about who he is and about how his people should pray and relate to him in this light. Sokolowski adds that the psalms "sketch a human possibility that is opened to us by the understanding of God that they help reveal: this is how we can take success, illness, defeat, or happiness, now that we believe that such things are part of what has been created by God."[23] That is, by giving his people these prayers and guiding their ongoing use as Scripture, God is continually informing his people about who he is, who his people are, and how they are to pray and relate to him and others.

A similar situation obtains with the Lord's Prayer. Jesus taught his disciples this prayer during his earthly ministry. After his death and resurrection, this prayer was preserved and transmitted as part

21. The Psalter as a whole is composed of "five books" or collections, each of which is marked off by a closing doxology: Pss. 1–41; 42–72; 73–89; 90–106; 107–150. A helpful introductory discussion is provided in Clifford, *Psalms 1–72*, 15–35.
22. Sokolowski, *Eucharistic Presence*, 152.
23. Sokolowski, *Eucharistic Presence*, 153.

of the apostolic teaching and became part of early Christian practice. In step with its preservation, transmission, and use in the early church, the Lord's Prayer came to be incorporated into the Gospels of Matthew and Luke, and these Gospels came to be recognized as the church's Scripture. It is as part of the church's Scripture and practice over time that the Lord's Prayer has come down to us today.

As both Scripture and an important part of Christian life, the Lord's Prayer serves the intellectual and practical formation of Christians. By giving this prayer to his disciples, Jesus is teaching us. He reveals things about the Father and, by implication, things about himself as the one who teaches this prayer. Moreover, Jesus also teaches his disciples about who they themselves are. By teaching us to address the Father as such and to ask him for certain things, the Lord's Prayer reveals to us our identity as children of the Father who also stand in need of things that only he can provide (hence, we petition him). By revealing truths about the Father, about Jesus, and about the disciples, the Lord's Prayer serves as an instrument by which the Lord forms us doctrinally.

In addition to providing doctrinal formation, the Lord's Prayer also serves the practical formation of the disciples. Jesus teaches his disciples how they are to relate to the Father by giving them a specific way to address God. By teaching us to pray for certain things, Jesus shows us those things for which we should be longing and praying. As Augustine writes, "The words our Lord Jesus Christ has taught us in his prayer give us the framework of true desires."[24] The Lord's Prayer also works to form Jesus's disciples practically by prescribing certain dispositions and ways of relating to others (e.g., forgiveness).

Since the divine economy of salvation also encompasses the ongoing life of the church, we are invited to receive Jesus's words as addressed to us in our present moment. When we receive Jesus's words in faith and make his words our own, the Lord is in that moment at work shaping us, bringing us more deeply into relation with his heavenly Father. When we pray the Lord's Prayer, not only are we

24. Augustine, *Essential Sermons* 56.5 (Hill, 86).

addressing the Father, but the Father is also addressing us through the words of his Son and forming us to live as his children.

The Lord's Prayer in the Context of Theology and Religious Practice

Eschatology

Another important matter of context is the conceptual setting for certain elements of the Lord's Prayer. This setting is the field of biblical teaching that we today call "eschatology." Coming from the Greek word *eschaton* ("last"), eschatology is theological teaching about ultimate or final things. With respect to the Bible, eschatology usually pertains to a definitive, saving act of God that he promises to work for his people at the end of days, thereby transforming the world and bringing his plans to completion.

Biblical eschatology is a broad category with a variety of forms (which are themselves not mutually exclusive). For instance, there is what is called restoration eschatology.[25] Arguably the most prominent form of eschatology in the Old Testament, this sort of teaching centers on God's end-time action to restore his people Israel from exile (i.e., the covenantal punishment for sin), an action that will impact the rest of the world.

As presented in the book of Deuteronomy, certain blessings and punishments were spelled out as following upon Israel's obedience or disobedience to the covenant. These are listed at length in Deuteronomy 28. The major covenantal punishment for sin is exile and scattering: God will break up the twelve tribes of Israel, expel them from the promised land, and subject them to the rule of the gentile nations (Deut. 28:63–64). Biblical texts present these covenantal punishments being enacted through the Assyrian conquest of the Northern Kingdom (722/721 BC; 2 Kings 17:1–23) and the Babylo-

---

25. See Petersen, "Eschatology," 2:575–79; Nickelsburg, "Eschatology (Early Jewish)," 2:579–94; Sanders, *Judaism*, 279–303.

nian conquest of the Southern Kingdom of Judah (587 BC; 2 Kings 25:8–21; 1 Chron. 9:1).

At the same time, the ever-faithful God also promises to restore his people who sincerely repent of their sins and obey him completely (Deut. 30:1–5). According to Deuteronomy 30, when this happens, "then the LORD your God will restore your fortunes and have compassion on you, gathering you again from all the people among whom the LORD your God has scattered you" (v. 3). Scenarios of restoration eschatology contain a variety of hopes and expectations for what this end-time action of God will involve. As noted by E. P. Sanders, among the most prominent and common expectations are the following: God will regather the twelve tribes of Israel and bring them back to the promised land; the gentile nations will variously be "converted, destroyed or subjugated"; "Jerusalem will be made glorious; the temple will be rebuilt, made more glorious or purified"; and "worship will be pure and the people will be righteous."[26] Within restoration eschatology, one also finds hope that God will raise up a righteous king in the line of David—that is, a messiah-king—to defeat his people's enemies and rule over restored Israel (Isa. 11:1–16; Jer. 33:14–26; Ezek. 37:24–25) and that God will permanently transform things into an ideal state, like a new garden of Eden (Isa. 51:3; Ezek. 36:35; 47:1–12).

Apocalypticism is another important form of biblical eschatology.[27] While conventionally associated with end-time destruction and cosmic upheavals, apocalypticism centers more on the revealing of heavenly truths and realities, sometimes referred to as "mysteries" (Dan. 2:28; cf. 2:17–23, 30).[28] These heavenly truths are revealed in highly symbolic visions, often through the mediation of an angel, and

26. Sanders, *Judaism*, 291–93.
27. Standard introductions to apocalypticism include Collins, *Apocalyptic Imagination*; Rowland, *Open Heaven*.
28. Christopher Rowland (*Open Heaven*, 11) writes, "The key to the whole [apocalyptic] movement is that God reveals his mysteries directly to man and thereby gives them knowledge of the true nature of reality so that they may organize their lives accordingly."

usually concern the cosmos and/or the course of history.[29] Apocalyptic eschatology often speaks to the people of God who are in the midst of crisis to reassure them that God is almighty and will ultimately secure justice in the world.

Apocalyptic scenarios that treat the course of history often frame things in a contrast between two cosmic states of affairs called ages. Illustrative of this thinking are the visions of the book of Daniel (and Dan. 7:1–14 in particular).[30] The present age is marked by sin, wickedness, injustice, and corruption. It is a cosmic state of affairs wherein the faithful people of God suffer at the hands of the wicked in power (7:1–8). At a spiritual level, the sin, wickedness, injustice, and corruption that mark the present age are connected to the spiritual powers of evil (i.e., the demonic), who have been granted a (limited) dominion over human beings and the world on account of sin. The problems of the present evil age become progressively worse, leading to an especially intense trial for God's people (the so-called messianic woes).[31] And then, God works his end-time saving act. In Daniel 7:9–12, God appears as the king and the judge. He defeats and condemns the powers of evil who oppose him and oppress his people. God's end-time action also involves the vindication of his faithful people, whom he resurrects to a glorified mode of life with him (cf. 12:2–3). As part of this definitive action to put all things right, God transforms the world into a permanent, perfected state of affairs: the future age to come. This future age to come is the eschatological state wherein God shares his kingly rule with his faithful people forever (7:13–14).

Much of Jesus's ministry fits within the horizon of biblical eschatology, and many elements in the Lord's Prayer allude to eschatological topics.[32] For instance, Jesus teaches about the kingdom of God

---

29. See Collins, *Apocalyptic Imagination*, 2–11.

30. On the influence of Daniel on subsequent apocalyptic thinking, see N. T. Wright, *New Testament*, 280–320.

31. See chap. 7 below.

32. See Meier, *Marginal Jew*, 2:291–302; N. T. Wright, "Lord's Prayer as a Paradigm," 132–54.

(Luke 4:43; cf. Matt. 4:17), and the Lord's Prayer features the petition "Your kingdom come" (Matt. 6:10; Luke 11:2). This teaching about God's end-time action as king and the related petition that God bring his kingdom to the world make sense within the eschatological teachings about God acting as the king in the end-time (e.g., Isa. 52:7–10; Dan. 2, 7; Zech. 14). As we will discuss, Jesus teaches that this eschatological action of God is in some respects present in him and his ministry and in other respects is something to be realized fully and plainly at a future time. Furthermore, the Lord's Prayer closes with petitions to the Father for help in "the time of trial" (*peirasmos*) and for "rescue . . . from the evil one" (Matt. 6:13). These petitions square with eschatological scenarios in which the end-time action of God is preceded by an intense period of suffering for God's people, a period that can have demonic associations. In short, as Jesus's ministry had a decidedly eschatological character to it, so too does the prayer he taught his disciples.

Ancient Jewish Prayer

Jesus was a Jewish man of the first century. Matthew and Luke present Jesus as doing all kinds of things that were part and parcel of Jewish religious life: he fasts and prays (Matt. 4:2 // Luke 4:2; Matt. 26:36–46 // Luke 22:39–46); he attends synagogue (Matt. 12:9; 13:54); he reads and comments on the Scripture (Luke 4:14–30); he debates Torah and its application with his contemporaries (Matt. 22:36–40; Luke 6:1–11); he goes on pilgrimage and participates in holy days (Matt. 21:1–11; Luke 9:51); when asked about the greatest of the commandments in Torah, he cites the Shema (Deut. 6:4) and the command to love one's neighbor (Lev. 19:18).

We should not be surprised, therefore, that the Lord's Prayer has some interesting similarities in wording, content, and expression with other Jewish prayers from antiquity. While these prayers underwent development of their own and are difficult to locate chronologically, they come from Jewish circles roughly contemporary with or somewhat later than Jesus's public ministry. For our purposes, these prayers illumine the religious world in which Jesus lived, and they help us to better understand the Lord's Prayer in its ancient religious context. There is an ancient Jewish prayer known as the Kaddish.[33] This Aramaic prayer seems to have originally followed a rabbinic sermon expounding the Scriptures. There are different forms of the Kaddish, and these forms serve different functions. One such version of the prayer reads as follows:

> May his great name be magnified and sanctified in the world that is to be created anew, when he will revive the dead, and raise them up unto life eternal, rebuild the city of Jerusalem, and establish his temple in the midst thereof, and uproot all alien worship from the earth and restore the worship of the true God. May the Holy One, blessed be he, establish his kingdom and his glory during your life and during your days, and during the life of all the house of Israel, and speedily and at a near time.[34]

Several similarities between the Kaddish and the Lord's Prayer stand out. The Kaddish opens "May his great name be magnified and sanctified," and the Lord's Prayer similarly contains the petition "Hallowed be your name" (Matt. 6:9; Luke 11:2). The Kaddish petitions God to "establish his kingdom," and the Lord's Prayer likewise asks "Your kingdom come" (Matt. 6:10; Luke 11:2). The Kaddish has an eschatological tone to it, asking the Lord to bring about the eschatological restoration, to resurrect the dead, and to rebuild Jerusalem and restore proper worship there. The Lord's Prayer similarly has an eschatological orientation, looking to the Father to bring his plan to its full completion (at Christ's return in glory).

Also significant is the set of Jewish prayers known as the Amidah or the Eighteen Benedictions.[35] The Amidah is a set of eighteen

---

33. On the background of the Kaddish, I follow Heinemann and Petuchowski, *Literature of the Synagogue*, 82–84.
34. Heinemann and Petuchowski, *Literature of the Synagogue*, 84.
35. On the Eighteen Benedictions, see Moore, *Judaism in the First Centuries*, 1:292–94; Mintz, "Prayer and the Prayerbook," 413–17; Heinemann and Petuchowski, *Literature of the Synagogue*, 29–36.

prayers and petitions that became a codified part of synagogue liturgy when the early rabbis were reconsolidating Jewish practice after the Roman destruction of the Jerusalem temple in AD 70. These liturgical prayers (or a selection of them) were to be prayed three times a day while standing.[36] This set of prayers as a whole follows a logic that starts by praising God and asking for forgiveness (prayers 1–3), then moves to making petitions for the individual and the nation (prayers 4–15), and concludes by offering thanksgiving (prayers 16–18).[37]

There are definite differences in form and content between the Eighteen Benedictions and the Lord's Prayer (esp. the length—the Lord's Prayer is much shorter), but as with the Kaddish, there are some interesting points of similarity.[38] For instance, petitions 4 and 6 address God directly as "our Father," as does Matthew's version of the Lord's Prayer. Petition 3 praises God's name, and petition 6 asks for God to forgive sins. Also like the Kaddish and the Lord's Prayer, many of the petitions in the Amidah have an eschatological tone to them. There are petitions that ask God to bring back Israel's exiles (9, 10), to bring about the restoration of the Davidic monarchy under the messiah-king (14), and to return to dwell in Zion (16).

These prayers from Jewish antiquity are inspiring expressions of piety and devotion to the Lord, and they have been recited by Jews in their worship of God down through the centuries. These Jewish prayers and the Lord's Prayer are different in some ways but similar in others. From a Christian perspective, these convergences and divergences should remind us of Jesus's own Jewishness and lead us to appreciate the genuine spiritual commonalities shared by Jews and Christians, who both, in respective ways, address the God of Israel in prayer as "our Father."

36. m. Ber. 2.4.
37. Moore, *Judaism in the First Centuries*, 1:293–94; Mintz, "Prayer and the Prayerbook," 415–17.
38. The text of the Amidah is cited from Heinemann and Petuchowski, *Literature of the Synagogue*, 33–36.

3

Conclusion

The Lord's Prayer has come down to us in the Gospels of Matthew and Luke. These two versions are similar in many ways, but they also have certain differences in language, content, and tone. Matthew and Luke also place the Lord's Prayer in different locations in their respective Gospel narratives. Each Gospel thus draws out different aspects of Jesus's teaching on prayer. The Lord's Prayer fits within the larger horizon of biblical prayer and pedagogy. Biblical prayer is our personal response to God, who has revealed himself to us. Through scriptural prayers in particular, God teaches us in a special way about himself and about ourselves, and he works to form our responses to him. Much in the Lord's Prayer resonates with elements of biblical eschatology, and it also has strong resonances with ancient Jewish prayers. As such, the Lord's Prayer is very much of a piece with the public ministry of Jesus, a Jewish man of the first century whose teaching was distinctly eschatological.

2

Our Father

The Lord's Prayer is a prayer to God the Father. Luke's version of the prayer opens with the simple address "Father" (11:2). Matthew gives a more developed (and familiar) form of the address: "Our Father in heaven" (6:9). Since the Lord's Prayer is addressed to the Father, each one of the prayer's petitions is a request that the Father act in some way. Through and through, the Lord's Prayer centers on the Father.

Jesus's teaching about the Father was an important and distinctive part of his ministry. In all four Gospels, Jesus refers to God as "Father" or "my Father" and speaks of himself as "the Son." The Gospels often present Jesus praying to God, and when we are given to know his prayers' contents, we see Jesus addressing God as "Father."[1] Jesus instructs his disciples along these same lines: God is their "Father," and when they pray, they too should address God with this name. And so, if we are to understand more deeply what it means to pray "our Father," we need to receive this prayer in light of what Jesus tells us about the Father and the relationship with the Father that he makes possible for us.

1. Matt. 11:25–27 // Luke 10:21–22; Matt. 26:36–46 // Mark 14:32–42 // Luke 22:39–46; Luke 23:34; John 11:41–42; 12:27–28; 17:1–26.

Since the Lord's Prayer centers on the Father, our study of the opening address, "our Father," will be more extensive than that of the individual petitions. This chapter has three major parts. The first part focuses on Jesus's teachings about the Father and involves the consideration of three related matters: (1) the ways God was called "Father" in the Old Testament and Jewish spirituality, (2) Jesus's teachings in Matthew and Luke about his relationship with the Father as the Son, and (3) Jesus's teachings about the Father and his ways toward people. The second part focuses on Jesus's incorporation of his disciples into his own relationship with the Father, both before and after the resurrection. The third part brings all these elements together and reflects in summary form on what it means to address God as "our Father" in the Lord's Prayer. In sum, when Christians pray "our Father," *we relate to the Father through our communion with Jesus his Son, which entails our communion with other members of the church, and through this prayer, Jesus invites us to know the Father's love and imitate his ways.*

Jesus Teaches about the Father

God as Father in the Old Testament and Ancient Jewish Spirituality

The identification of the God of Israel as Father (Hb. *'āb*; Gk. *patēr*) appears in a modest number of passages in the Old Testament as well as in some other ancient Jewish writings and prayers close to Jesus's day.[2] While Jesus was not the first person to call God "Father," he did so with great frequency and in some distinctive ways. We can acquire more insight into Jesus's teaching about the Father by examining other uses of this address in the biblical tradition as well as topics associated with it (e.g., the relationships between fathers and their children).

2. There are roughly twenty to thirty occurrences, depending on whether one includes the Deuterocanonical books. Jonathan Pennington provides a helpful inventory of uses in the apocrypha and pseudepigrapha in his *Heaven and Earth*, 219n8.

God as Father in Biblical Texts and Traditions

The most prominent way in which God is presented as Father in the Old Testament is his being the father of the people Israel. God becomes the father of Israel when he chooses them as his special people and enters into a covenant relationship with them.

Old Testament texts often present God as the father of Israel in connection with the events of the exodus. When God first appears to Moses and calls him to be his instrument in the exodus, he instructs Moses to say the following to Pharaoh: "Thus says the LORD: Israel is my firstborn son. I said to you, 'Let my son go that he may worship me'" (Exod. 4:22–23; cf. Deut. 14:1; Mal. 2:10). Similarly, the prophet Hosea associates God's being the father of Israel with his action to save them in the exodus and care for them. Through the prophet, the Lord says, "When Israel was a child, I loved him, and out of Egypt I called my son. . . . Yet it was I who taught Ephraim to walk. . . . I was to them like those who lift infants to their cheeks. I bent down to them and fed them" (Hosea 11:1, 3–4). The Song of Moses in Deuteronomy 32:1–43 likewise speaks of the Lord as the "father" of Israel (32:6), who chose them as his special people, protected and cared for them in the wilderness (32:9–12), and brought them to the promised land (32:13–14).

Throughout the Bible, the exodus from Egypt provides a model for God's saving action. Accordingly, when prophets announce that God will work a new, definitive saving act at the end of days, they often employ the language and imagery of the exodus to present this end-time saving action as a new exodus.[3] In this eschatological new exodus, God will show himself to be Israel's father as he forgives his people their sins and brings them back from their exilic punishment.[4] Speaking of this future action, the Lord says through Jeremiah, "With

---

3. On the typological use of the exodus motif to talk about the eschatological act of God, see Fishbane, *Biblical Text and Texture*, 121–40.

4. In Deut. 32, Moses scolds the Israelites for their unfaithfulness and disobedience to God their "father," who has shown them his goodness in the past and promises to deliver them powerfully again in the future (vv. 4–5). A similar connection of God's end-time saving action with his being the father of Israel appears in Jub. 1:23–25.

consolations I will lead them back . . . ; for I have become a father to Israel, and Ephraim is my firstborn" (Jer. 31:9). The text later adds, "Is Ephraim my dear son? . . . I am deeply moved for him; I will surely have mercy on him, says the LORD" (31:20).

The Scriptures also present God as being the father of select individuals. This is the case in God becoming the adoptive father of the Davidic king. In the Davidic covenant oracle of 2 Samuel 7, the Lord promises David that he will never reject the Davidic line of kings. When speaking of David's future heir, the Lord says of him, "I will be a father to him, and he shall be a son to me" (2 Sam. 7:14; cf. 1 Chron. 17:13; 22:10; 28:10). This same bit of royal theology appears in Psalm 2. Here the psalmist speaks of God adopting the Davidic king as a son: "I will tell of the decree of the LORD: He said to me, 'You are my son; today I have begotten you'" (2:7). Similar to his being the father of Israel, God is the father of the Davidic king through his *choosing* of David's royal line and thus the occupant of its throne.

The book of Wisdom speaks of God as the father of the righteous person. Wisdom 2:12–20 depicts a group of wicked people who are heaping scorn on a righteous man whom they resent. The righteous person "professes to have knowledge of God and calls himself a child of the Lord" (Wis. 2:13). Plotting the death of the righteous man, the wicked say of him, he "boasts that God is his father. . . . Let us test what will happen at the end of his life; for if the righteous man is God's child [lit., son], he will help him" (2:16, 18; cf. Matt. 27:43). Interestingly, this text from Wisdom foregrounds a different aspect of the father-child relationship between God and a human being. In the case of the people Israel and the Davidic king, God's being their father is grounded in his choosing them. In Wisdom 2, God is the father of the righteous person because the righteous person lives a righteous life—that is, this person knows the ways of the Lord and obeys him.

To understand better the presentation of God as father in relation to his children, it is helpful to consider these relationships in light of what the biblical witness says about the ideal relation between human fathers and their sons. As we shall see, biblical texts align these relationships in mutually illuminating ways.

Fathers and Children

Human Fathers and Children

George Foot Moore spells out the basic responsibilities of a father to his son in the biblical tradition: in addition "to support[ing] his children during their early years . . . he must circumcise him, redeem him, teach him Torah, teach him a trade, and get him a wife."[5] For our purposes, we will highlight three responsibilities that a father has toward his child, and then we will examine the responsibilities of children to their parents.

First, a father loves his children and provides for them. The Old Testament writings employ a variety of words for love.[6] The Hebrew verb 'āhab ("to love") is often used in the context of parent-child relationships, articulating Abraham's love for Isaac (Gen. 22:2), Isaac's love for Esau and Rebekah's love for Jacob (25:28), and Jacob's love for Joseph (37:3). In such uses, the term connotes affection, kindness, tender care, and attachment.

Second, a father has a responsibility to teach his children. Most importantly, a father was to teach his children the Torah and the sacred traditions of Israel.[7] In the Shema (Deut. 6:4–9), Moses directs Israel: "Keep these words. . . . Recite them to your children and talk about them" (vv. 6–7). Exodus contains several places that speak of parents handing on to their children the words and deeds of the Lord and explaining their significance (10:2; 12:26–27; 13:8; cf. Josh. 4:21–24; Ps. 78:3–4). Additionally, a father was to teach his son a trade (or arrange for him to be taught a trade). Such training would enable his son to make a living and thus be able to support a family of his own. Reviewing pertinent evidence from Jewish and non-Jewish

5. Moore, *Judaism in the First Centuries*, 2:127.
6. See Sakenfeld, "Love (Old Testament)," 4:374–81.
7. De Vaux, *Ancient Israel*, 1:49.

sources, C. H. Dodd points out that in this educational process an apprenticed son would watch his father/teacher and learn to follow his example.[8] According to Dodd, observation and imitation of the father are central in this process: *the son learns from and imitates the ways of the father.*[9]

Third, the father has the responsibility to form his children's moral character through correction and discipline. Proverbs 3:12 holds that a father's correcting of his child is an expression of his love for his child. The book of Sirach speaks (albeit harshly) of a father's obligation to form properly his son's moral character through discipline (30:1–6). A wise and virtuous father trains a son to be similarly wise and virtuous. When the father dies, "he will not seem to be dead, for he has left behind him one like himself" (30:4). Similarly, the book of Tobit voices the association between a good father (Tobias) and his good son (Tobit): "Good and noble son of a father good and noble, upright and generous" (9:6). Both Sirach and Tobit speak of a good son as an image that reflects his father's own goodness.

Children, for their part, had obligations and responsibilities toward their parents. These are summarized in the commandment "Honor your father and your mother" (Deut. 5:16; cf. Exod. 20:12; Lev. 19:3). Honoring one's parents entails a variety of attitudes and actions. For instance, Sirach 3:1–16 unpacks the commandment to honor one's parents by commending "respect" (3:6), good words and conduct (3:8), caring for one's parents, especially when elderly and infirm (3:12–13), maintaining the bonds of family attachment (3:16), and showing "kindness" (3:14). Proverbs encourages children to be docile and take in their parents' instructions (1:8; 2:1; 3:1; 4:10, 20).[10] The author encourages a child to watch and learn to imitate the father's good conduct (23:26) like an apprentice learning a craft from a teacher.

8. Dodd, "Hidden Parable," 32–39.
9. The association of fatherhood with teaching shaped the practice of speaking about the teacher-student relationship in terms of father and son.
10. Jon Levenson (*Love of God*, 20) notes the linguistic and thematic similarities between the Shema and texts in Proverbs that exhort a son to hear his father's instructions (e.g., Prov. 1:8; 5:1, 7; 7:24; 23:19).

An especially important way in which children love and honor their parents is through their obedience. Proverbs 6:20 expressly states, "My child, keep your father's commandment, and do not forsake your mother's teaching." Later, the author makes a similar statement: "My child, keep my words and store up my commandments with you; keep my commandments and live" (7:1–2). Another way in which the Torah points to the importance of children to obey and so honor their parents is by spelling out punishments for disobedience or violence against parents (Exod. 21:15, 17; Deut. 21:18–21).

God as Father and the Israelites as His Children

The biblical tradition closely aligns the relationship of parents and children with that of God and his children. Moore observes, "The Scripture employs the same expressions about honoring, revering, cursing parents as about honoring, revering, or cursing [God], thus . . . equating the things themselves."[11] God loves and provides for his people, gives them the Torah, and disciplines them to form their character. Similarly, human fathers were to love their children, teach them the Torah, and form their conduct through correction. As God's children were to learn from, imitate, and obey him, so children were to learn from, imitate, and obey their parents.

A human father "loves" (Hb. 'āhab) his children, and God similarly "loves" his people (Hb. 'āhab; Deut. 4:37; Isa. 43:4). He shows them his "compassion" (Hb. rāḥam) and "loving-kindness" (Hb. ḥesed).[12] God manifests his fatherhood in his benevolent, protective care for his people, especially the most needy and vulnerable: he is "Father of orphans and protector of widows" (Ps. 68:5). He is the good father to the child who does not have one and the protector of the widow who could not participate in public life in ancient Israel. Psalm 103

11. Moore, *Judaism in the First Centuries*, 2:131. This alignment appears (albeit in negative terms) in Mal. 1:6. Here, the Lord reprimands the priests of Judah for disobeying his instructions for how to offer proper worship: "A son honors his father, and servants their master. If then I am a father, where is the honor due me?" Judah's disobedient priests are equated with sons who disobey (and thus dishonor) their father.

12. Sakenfeld, "Love (Old Testament)," 4:376–80.

likens God's tender care for his people to that of a father for his children: "As a father has compassion for his children, so the LORD has compassion for those who fear him" (v. 13; cf. Job 31:18). As father, God is a source of strength and help for people in need. The Davidic king addresses God, "You are my Father, my God, and the Rock of my salvation!" (Ps. 89:26).

As a good father, God wants his children to be good—that is, to be faithful and obedient to him and so honor him. Deuteronomy frequently articulates the covenant relationship of God and Israel in terms of father and son (1:31; 14:1; 32:5–6). Within these terms, Deuteronomy commends Israel to love and obey the Lord as a son should love and obey his father. In the Shema, Israel is instructed, "You shall love [Hb. 'āhab] the LORD your God with all your heart, and with all your soul, and with all your might" (6:5). Deuteronomy goes on to specify that Israel's love and affection for the Lord is lived out in obedience.[13] As Moses says to Israel, "If you obey the commandments of the LORD your God . . . by loving the LORD your God, walking in his ways, and observing his commandments, decrees, and ordinances, then you shall live" (30:16; cf. 10:12–13; 11:1, 22). As a child loves his father by learning from and obeying him, so too the people Israel love the Lord by taking in his Torah and obeying him.

God's fatherhood also involves correcting and disciplining his children when they do wrong. Deuteronomy makes this claim plainly and does so with appeal to the relation between father and child: "Know then in your heart that as a parent disciplines a child so the LORD your God disciplines you" (8:5). In the Davidic covenant oracle, God says that he will discipline the king (his adopted "son") for wrongdoing but will not "take my steadfast love from him" (2 Sam. 7:15). This association of God's fatherhood with the parental responsibility of disciplining children for bad behavior likewise appears in Proverbs: "My child, do not despise the LORD's discipline or be wary of his reproof, for the LORD reproves the one he loves, as a father the son in

---

13. Moran, "Ancient Near Eastern Background," 77–87; Levenson, *Love of God*, 3–10; Sakenfeld, "Love (Old Testament)," 4:376.

whom he delights" (3:11–12; cf. Wis. 11:10). As a good father, God acts to correct his children's bad behavior (including through negative reinforcement) so as to facilitate the formation of good character.

Addressing God as "Father" in Prayer

We also see God addressed (or identified) as "Father" in some Jewish prayers from the time before and shortly after Jesus's earthly life. The book of Tobit contains a prayer that calls on Israel to praise God "because he is our Lord and he is our God; he is our Father and he is God forever" (13:4). Similarly, Sirach invokes God, "O Lord, Father and Master of my life" (23:1), and asks him for help in resisting temptations to sin, especially sins of speech, lust, and gluttony (cf. 23:4). Sirach later recounts that when facing a variety of mortal dangers, he turned to God for help, saying, "Lord, you are my Father" (51:10). He goes on to praise God for having heard his prayer and rescuing him (51:12).[14]

Among the Dead Sea Scrolls, there is some evidence for God being identified as "Father" in prayer. One of the thanksgiving hymns (1QH^a col. 17, line 35) says of God, "You are father to all the [son]s of your truth."[15] In fragments from a text called The Apocryphon of Joseph, the patriarch Joseph is given to say, "My father and my God, do not abandon me into the hands of gentiles" (4Q372 frag. 1, col. 16).[16]

Other important Jewish prayers associated with the synagogue liturgy (introduced in the previous chapter) similarly address God as "Father." In the Amidah, the Lord is addressed as "our Father" in petitions 4 and 6. The fourth benediction praises God for teaching Israel his Torah: "Graciously favor us, our Father, with understanding from thee, And discernment and insight out of thy Torah.

14. Other Second Temple Jewish writings wherein God is addressed as "father" in prayer are Jos. Asen. 12:8; 3 Macc. 6:8.
15. García Martínez and Tigchelaar, *Dead Sea Scrolls*, 1:185.
16. García Martínez and Tigchelaar, *Dead Sea Scrolls*, 2:736–37. See also 4Q460 frag. 5, col. 5.

Blessed art thou, O Lord, gracious bestower of understanding."[17] A father's sacred responsibility is to instruct his children in the commandments of the Lord (e.g., Deut. 6:4–9; Prov. 1:8; 4:1–4), and similarly here, God is called "Father" in that he teaches his wisdom and ways to Israel, his child. The sixth petition also calls God "Father" as it asks God to forgive sins: "Forgive us, our Father, for we have sinned against thee, Erase and blot out our transgressions from before thine eyes, For thou art abundantly compassionate. Blessed art thou, O Lord, who forgivest readily."[18] This address of God as "Father" recalls Psalm 103, which says that God "forgives all . . . iniquity" and has compassion for his people as a father has compassion for his children (vv. 3, 13).

Addressing God as "Father" in connection with his love, teaching, and mercy are similarly combined in a prayer known as the Ahabah Rabbah (or "Great Love"). Referencing Jeremiah 31:3, the prayer begins, "With abounding . . . love, hast Thou loved us, O Lord our God. With great and exceeding compassion hast Thou taken compassion on us."[19] The text continues, "Our Father, our King, . . . be gracious unto us, and be Thou also our teacher. Enlighten our eyes in Thy law, and make our hearts cleave to Thy commandments; render our hearts one that we may love and fear Thy name."[20] As in the Amidah, God is called "Father" for his love and compassion and his teaching Israel his Torah.

Having examined these witnesses, we can see that when Jesus speaks about the Father and teaches his disciples to address God as "Father" in prayer, he does so in ways that are at home in the biblical tradition and Jewish piety. At the same time, as we now turn to examine Jesus's teaching about the Father, we see that Jesus employs these traditional elements in ways that are his own and introduces a way of addressing the Father that (as far as we know) is unique.

17. Heinemann and Petuchowski, *Literature of the Synagogue*, 34.
18. Heinemann and Petuchowski, *Literature of the Synagogue*, 34.
19. Kohler, "Ahabah Rabbah."
20. Kohler, "Ahabah Rabbah."

The Father and the Son

When we read the Gospels, it is striking just how often Jesus calls God "Father." Jesus sometimes speaks of the deity simply as "God." Beyond that, Jesus uses the word "Father" to refer to God far more often than any other title or epithet. By my count, of all the places in the Gospels where Jesus speaks directly about God (and is not quoting Scripture), there are only about five instances where Jesus refers to God with a title other than "Father."[21] So while "Father" was an attested name (among others) for God in the Scriptures and in Jewish piety around his time, Jesus makes "Father" the central and predominant name for God in his teaching.

Jesus teaches that he has a unique and intimate relationship with the Father. Throughout the Gospels, Jesus calls God "my Father" and similarly refers to himself as "the Son."[22] Just as there is precedent for pious Jews to call God "Father," so also is there precedent for thinking of a "son" of God (e.g., the people Israel, the Davidic king, or a righteous or wise person).[23] Yet when Jesus speaks of himself as the Son of the Father, he claims a status and a relationship with the Father that exceed what other instances of these phrases claim.

We will, therefore, examine passages from the Gospels of Matthew and Luke that display Jesus's relationship with the Father. Having a sense for the nature of Jesus's relationship with the Father will enable us to grasp what it is for Jesus to teach his disciples to refer to God as their Father.

21. Jesus refers to God by other epithets in these references: "Lord" (Mark 13:20; possibly Mark 5:19); "Most High" (Luke 6:35); "Creator" (Matt. 19:4); "Great King" (Matt. 5:35); "The Power" (Mark 14:62 // Matt. 26:64).

22. Jesus speaks of God as "my Father" in these places: Matt. 7:21; 10:32–33; 11:27; 12:50; 15:13; 16:17; 18:10, 19, 35; 20:23; 25:34; 26:29, 39, 42, 53; Luke 10:22; 22:29; 24:49. While others speak of Jesus as "the Son" in the Gospels of Matthew and Luke, Jesus speaks of himself as "the Son" in these places: Matt. 11:27; 24:36; 28:19; Luke 10:22. He also implies himself to be the son in the parable of the wicked tenants (Matt. 21:33–46 // Luke 20:9–19).

23. There are also places in Scripture where angels are referred to as "sons" of God or of heaven (e.g., Gen. 6:2; Job 2:1; 38:7; cf. Ps. 82:6–7).

Jesus, the Son of the Father from the Beginning of His Life

Both Matthew and Luke establish that Jesus is the divine Son of God from the beginning of his life. These Gospels make this point in the narrative sections that precede Jesus's public ministry.

Of the four New Testament Gospels, only Matthew and Luke contain an infancy narrative that presents Jesus's birth and youth. Despite their differences in tone and content and their having most likely been composed independently of each other, these two infancy narratives agree on a number of salient points.[24] One such point of agreement is that Jesus is the Son of God on account of his virginal conception; that is, Matthew and Luke independently present Mary as conceiving Jesus through the creative power of the Holy Spirit and in a nonsexual way (Matt. 1:20; Luke 1:35), and they agree that Jesus's identity as the Son of God follows upon the virginal conception.[25]

Matthew interprets the virginal conception of Jesus in light of Isaiah 7:14 LXX. On account of his being conceived by the Virgin Mary through the Spirit's power, Jesus is identified as "Emmanuel," meaning that he is "God with us" (Matt. 1:23 alt.). When Matthew later narrates the holy family's flight into Egypt, he interprets this event with a quotation from Hosea 11:1: "Out of Egypt I have called my son" (Matt. 2:15). Matthew reads Hosea as the direct discourse of God (the Father), who calls Jesus his "son." The term "son" here, in one sense, identifies Jesus as the personification of the people Israel, who are corporately God's son (and who similarly came out of Egypt in the exodus). But given what Matthew has already said about Jesus's

---

24. For a helpful index of these points of agreement, see Brown, *Birth of the Messiah*, 34–35.

25. That the virginal conception of Jesus by Mary is a nonsexual (and miraculous) occurrence is suggested by the words of Gabriel to Mary in Luke 1:35. Gabriel's words connect the conception of Jesus to the glory of the Lord coming to dwell in the wilderness tabernacle. He tells Mary, "The power of the Most High will overshadow [*episkiasei*] you," and the verb *episkiazō* recalls the descent of the glory into the tabernacle: "Moses was not able to enter the tent of meeting because the cloud settled upon it [LXX: *epeskiazen*], and the glory of the LORD filled the tabernacle" (Exod. 40:35). Typologically, as the glory of the Lord (the manifest presence of God) descends to dwell in the tabernacle, so does the deity comparably descend to become human in the Virgin Mary's womb.

human origins, the term "son" here also includes reference to Jesus's divine identity as Emmanuel. Jesus is the Father's Son from the very beginning of his human existence. Whereas the people Israel and the Davidic king are God's son by his choosing them, Jesus is God's Son by generation and also by virtue of his personifying faithful Israel in his humanity.

Luke's infancy narrative makes this connection between Jesus's divine Sonship and the virginal conception even more overt. When Mary asks the angel Gabriel how what he has announced will come about, given her virginity, Gabriel replies, "The Holy Spirit will come upon you, and the power of the Most High will overshadow you; therefore, the holy one born will also be called Son of God" (Luke 1:35 alt.).[26] Important for our purposes is the word "therefore" (dio). Mary's conceiving Jesus by the power of the Holy Spirit provides the reason on account of which (i.e., "therefore") Jesus "will also be called Son of God." Jesus's identity as the Son of God follows on his being conceived by the power of the Holy Spirit in Mary's womb. As in Matthew, the title "Son of God" in Luke signifies Jesus's divine identity from the first moment of his life.

Luke expands this point in the last episode of his infancy narrative, the scene in which Mary and Joseph find twelve-year-old Jesus in the Jerusalem temple (2:41–51). After Mary and Joseph find young Jesus in the temple after a three-day search, Mary asks Jesus, "Child, why have you treated us like this? Look, your father and I have been searching for you in great anxiety" (2:48). When Mary speaks to Jesus of "your father," she has in mind Joseph, Jesus's adoptive father. Jesus's reply to her is significant: "Why were you searching for me? Did you not know that I must be in my Father's house?" (2:49). While Mary uses the word "father" to mean Joseph, Jesus uses the phrase "my Father" to refer to God. These are the very first words that Jesus speaks in the Gospel of Luke. In them, we are given to see that Jesus, even at twelve years old, has an awareness of his relation to God the Father as his Son.

26. I thank Nathan Eubank for his insight on a grammatical matter here.

Matthew and Luke continue their exposition of Jesus's divine Sonship in their accounts of his baptism (Matt. 3:13–17; Luke 3:21–22).[27] Significant for our purposes are the words of the Father spoken from heaven after Jesus is baptized. Though there are some differences between Matthew and Luke as to each's framing of the statement, the voice from heaven declares Jesus to be "my Son, the Beloved," and one with whom the Father is "well pleased" (Matt. 3:17; Luke 3:22).[28] These words of the Father draw from several Scripture passages and associate Jesus with a variety of Old Testament figures, such as the Davidic king, Isaac, and the servant of the Lord in Isaiah 40–55.[29] But given what Matthew and Luke have already set forth in their infancy narratives, the Father's declaration that Jesus is "my Son" entails Jesus's divine identity. Identifying Jesus as the Son may include more than his divinity, but it does not include less.

To use the language of Christian doctrine, the infancy narratives teach us that Jesus is the Father's Son by nature and not by adoption or imitation. That is to say, Jesus does not "become" the Father's Son by being adopted or chosen by him. Rather, Jesus is the Son from the first moment of his human existence, the moment of his conception (and indeed, within the Trinity, the Son is eternally and timelessly begotten by the Father). As we turn to teachings of Jesus from his public ministry, we will see him suggesting that his relationship with the Father is heavenly in nature. Such statements, combined with other testimony from the New Testament, display the mystery of

27. The evangelists' exposition of Jesus's divine Sonship in the prepublic ministry material also appears in their narratives of Jesus's temptations (Matt. 4:1–11 // Luke 4:1–13). See chap. 7 below.

28. Matthew frames the Father's words as a public revelation, for it is articulated in the third person: "This is my Son, the Beloved, with whom I am well pleased" (Matt. 3:17). Luke, however, presents the Father's words as spoken to Jesus himself, for the statement uses the second person "you": "You are my Son, the Beloved, with you I am well pleased" (Luke 3:22).

29. The Father's words at Jesus's baptism include allusions: "You are my son" quotes Ps. 2:7, alluding to the Davidic king; the specification that Jesus is the "beloved son" recalls Isaac, who is similarly called in Gen. 22:2, 12, 16; the phrase "well pleased" alludes to the servant of the Lord in Isa. 42:1: "Here is my servant, whom I uphold, my chosen, in whom my soul delights."

the incarnation defined by the creeds and early church councils: the eternal Son of God becomes fully human without any diminishment of his divinity in Jesus of Nazareth.[30]

Jesus, the Son of the Father: Witness from His Public Ministry

Turning to Gospel narratives of Jesus's public ministry, we will examine four passages that display Jesus's relationship with the Father. First, both Matthew and Luke present Jesus offering a prayer of thanksgiving to the Father in which he praises the Father for those who have received his teaching (Matt. 11:25–27 // Luke 10:21–22). Given its importance, we quote the passage in full: "I thank you, Father, Lord of heaven and earth, because you have hidden these things from the wise and the intelligent and have revealed them to infants; yes, Father, for such was your gracious will. All things have been handed over to me by my Father; and no one knows the Son except the Father, and no one knows the Father except the Son and anyone to whom the Son chooses to reveal him" (Matt. 11:25–27).

In these words, Jesus claims to have a unique relationship with God, whom he calls "my Father" (Matt. 11:27). This relationship is one of familial closeness and intimate knowing: the Father "knows" the Son, and the Son "knows" the Father (11:27; cf. John 10:14–15). Furthermore, this relationship between the Father and the Son is unique to them, for "only" the Father and the Son know each other in this way.

30. In 451, the Council of Chalcedon formally defined the mystery of the incarnation:
> Following therefore the holy Fathers, we unanimously teach to confess one and the same Son, our Lord Jesus Christ, the same perfect in divinity and perfect in humanity, the same truly God and truly man composed of rational soul and body, the same one in being with the Father as to the divinity and one in being with us as to the humanity, like unto us in all things but sin [cf. Heb. 4:15]. The same was begotten from the Father before the ages as to the divinity and in the latter days for us and our salvation was born as to his humanity from Mary the Virgin Mother of God. (Denzinger, *Compendium of Creeds*, §301 [p. 109])

With the statement "All things have been handed over to me by my Father" (Matt. 11:27), Jesus says that the Father has given him the unique authority and prerogative to teach. Used in this context, the verb for "handed over" (*paradidōmi*) recalls the technical language in Jewish tradition for the transmission and reception of teaching.[31] Since only Jesus has this unique relationship with the Father as his Son, Jesus is uniquely able to reveal the Father to people: "No one knows the Father except the Son and anyone to whom the Son chooses to reveal him" (11:27). Hence, Jesus praises the Father that his words have found a favorable reception among some people, whom he calls here the "infants." These are the ones who receive what the Father has "revealed" because they receive Jesus's words (11:25).

Jesus's words about himself as the Son echo things said in ancient Jewish literature about the Wisdom or Word of God as a heavenly figure. For instance, Jesus says that "no one knows the Father except the Son" (Matt. 11:27). Similarly, Wisdom 9 says that God's personified Wisdom, who exists in heaven with God, knows him: "She . . . knows your works . . . understands what is pleasing in your sight . . . [and] knows and understands all things" (vv. 9, 11). Jesus, given his unique, intimate knowledge of the Father as the Son, is alone able to reveal the Father (Matt. 11:27). Similarly, in Wisdom 9, Solomon prays that God would send his Wisdom into the world to make God's ways known to people: "Send her forth from the holy heavens, and from the throne of your glory send her, . . . that I may learn what is pleasing to you" (v. 10; cf. 8:4; 9:17–18). In light of such allusions to God's Wisdom, Jesus seems to be implicitly identifying himself here as the Word or Wisdom of God in the flesh.[32] As such, Jesus knows the Father in a way that no one else does, and on the basis of his unique relationship with the Father, Jesus alone can make the Father known in a unique, unparalleled way.

31. See Jeremias, *Prayers of Jesus*, 49; Gerhardsson, *Memory and Manuscript*, 289.

32. For discussion, see Harrington, *Gospel of Matthew*, 166–70; Davies and Allison, *Gospel according to Saint Matthew*, 2:272, 291–93, 295–97; Keener, *Historical Jesus*, 273–74.

A second text that speaks to Jesus's relationship with the Father is the parable of the wicked tenants (Matt. 21:33–46 // Luke 20:9–19). This parable is a prophetic indictment of the Jerusalem authorities, and Jesus tells this parable in Jerusalem in the last week of his public ministry. In this parable, Jesus rehearses the history of Israel ("the vineyard").[33] He aligns its current and past leadership ("the tenants"), who have rejected and maltreated the prophets ("the servants") whom God ("the owner") sent to them. After sending a series of servants, the owner decides to send his "son," whom the tenants take out of the vineyard and kill (Matt. 21:39 // Luke 20:15). As N. T. Wright observes, the ending of this parable segues into Jesus's subsequent words about the building of a new eschatological temple by way of Psalm 118:22 (and some wordplay in the underlying Hebrew language). For the rejected "son" (Hb. *bēn*) becomes "the stone" (Hb. *'eben*) of a new edifice built by God.[34]

Much as Jesus implicitly identifies Israel's leadership of his day with the tenants in the parable, so too does he identify himself with the owner's son in the parable. As the owner's son, Jesus is both like and unlike the biblical prophets. Like the prophets, Jesus is "sent" by God to Israel and its leadership, and indeed, he is the final one to be sent to them (Matt. 21:34, 36–37). But Jesus is also categorically different from the prophets. The last one in the series of those sent is not one of the servants. Rather, he is the owner's son (21:37), and as such, he exists in a different kind of relationship with the owner/God. In this way, Jesus presents himself as something more than and different from a prophet. Jesus's unique status is one of the elements contained in his being the son.

Third, there is a saying in Matthew's (and Mark's) account of Jesus's apocalyptic discourse in which Jesus says that he does not know the specific time of the present world's end: "But about that day and hour no one knows, neither the angels of heaven, nor the Son,

33. The vineyard is an important biblical image for the people Israel. See Ps. 80:8–19; Isa. 5:1–7.
34. Following here N. T. Wright, *Jesus and the Victory*, 497–501.

but only the Father" (Matt. 24:36 // Mark. 13:32). While one could read these words and focus on a limitation of Jesus's knowledge, this saying does in fact point to an extraordinary status for Jesus as the Son.[35] The saying operates with a kind of ascending dynamic as to who does and does not know the day and hour. It begins with a generic "no one" (which arguably includes all human beings) and then ascends to the angels, then to the Son, and then to the Father, who alone knows. This ascending order points to Jesus the Son as having a status and a relation to the Father that are superior to those of "the angels of heaven." Similar to Jesus's prayer of thanksgiving discussed above, this is a subtle affirmation that Jesus's relationship with the Father is heavenly. As the Son, Jesus claims to be superior to the angels and closer to the Father than they are.

Fourth, there is Jesus's prayer in Gethsemane (Matt. 26:36–46 // Mark 14:32–42 // Luke 22:39–46). All the Gospels (including John in his own way) present Jesus addressing God as "Father" in his prayer before his arrest (Matt. 26:39 // Mark 14:36 // Luke 22:42; cf. John 12:27–28). Mark preserves the Aramaic word that Jesus uses to address God: "Abba" (14:36). The word 'abbā' is an emphatic form of the ordinary word for father in both Hebrew and Aramaic, 'ab.[36]

It has been argued that 'abbā' is what a child would affectionately call his or her father (akin to the English word "dad").[37] While this is possible, the evidence cited for this conclusion comes from sources later than the New Testament.[38] In evidence closer to the time of Jesus, 'abbā' was used by adults to refer to their fathers, and in the Mishnah, 'abbā' serves as an honorary title for a distinguished rabbi or teacher.[39]

35. Cf. Brown, *Introduction to New Testament Christology*, 56–58, 89.
36. Fitzmyer, "*Abba* and Jesus' Relation," 17.
37. This was argued by Joachim Jeremias in an essay, contained in the volume *Prayers of Jesus*, 11–65. For a helpful critique (and tempering) of Jeremias's argument, see Barr, "'Abbā Isn't 'Daddy.'"
38. Jeremias (*Prayers of Jesus*, 59, 61) appeals to two key texts from the Babylonian Talmud: b. Ber. 40a and b. Ta'an. 23b.
39. Joseph Fitzmyer ("*Abba* and Jesus' Relation," 21) cites inscriptional evidence on several ossuaries (i.e., burial boxes) where a deceased father is called "abba." For

Indeed, James Barr states that *'abbā'* would have been a regular term by which adults referred to their own fathers.[40]

Given that the word *'abbā'* was used by adult children for their fathers or for a revered teacher (as noted above, teachers were regarded as father figures), the word *'abbā'* connotes devotion, affection, and respect. There is no case, however, of *'abbā'* ever being used as an address for God before Jesus. As Joseph Fitzmyer concludes, "There is no evidence in the literature of pre-Christian or first-century Palestinian Judaism that *'abbā'* was used in any sense as a personal address for God by an individual—and for Jesus to address God as *'abbā'* or 'Father' is therefore something new."[41]

Jesus's practice of calling God "Father" and his use of the term *'abbā'* had a major impact on his disciples. Paul retains the Aramaic word *'abbā'* when he writes about the baptized coming to share in Jesus's own relationship with the Father (Rom. 8:15; Gal 4:6). Moreover, every single New Testament writing (except 3 John) follows Jesus's practice by referring to God as "Father" or, more specifically, as Jesus's Father. Such widespread use of the name "Father" for God in the New Testament writings shows how directive was Jesus's own teaching and practice on the early Christians.

As we will again discuss in chapter 7, in the Gethsemane prayer, Jesus shows himself to be the Father's Son through his love, commitment, and obedience to the Father. As we have seen, in the biblical tradition a good child honors his father by learning from him and obeying his instructions (Prov. 4:4–5, 20–21; 6:20; 7:1–3). Deuteronomy similarly teaches that Israel (as a child) loves the Lord (as Father) by obeying him. By submitting to the Father's will for him and repeatedly praying "Your will be done" (Matt. 26:42), Jesus shows himself to be the Father's obedient Son. Indeed, as Luke's passion narrative highlights, Jesus exemplifies trusting obedience to his Father unto

examples of "abba" used to address a revered teacher, see m. Shabb. 24.5; m. Qidd. 4.14; m. Avot 2.8.

40. Barr, "'Abbā Isn't 'Daddy,'" 35–37.
41. Fitzmyer, "*Abba* and Jesus' Relation," 28.

the end of his life. This is manifest in Jesus's dying words, a quote from Psalm 31:5: "Father, into your hands I commend my spirit" (Luke 23:46). Jesus's obedience, especially in his suffering and death, expresses the depth of his own love and commitment to the Father.

To sum up, when Jesus speaks of God as his Father and himself as the Son, he claims to have a unique relationship with the Father. His status as the Son distinguishes him from the biblical prophets, and in his ministry, he subtly indicates that his relationship with the Father is heavenly. The infancy narratives of Matthew and Luke support this point by associating Jesus's divine Sonship with his virginal conception. In his public ministry, Jesus displays his divine Sonship not only by revealing the Father but also by his total love and obedience toward the Father.

Knowing the Father

There are several passages in Matthew and Luke in which Jesus tells us about the Father and his ways toward people. Of particular importance are Jesus's love command (Matt. 5:43–48 // Luke 6:27–36), Jesus's teaching about the Father's generous providing (Matt. 6:25–34 // Luke 12:22–34), and a passage where Jesus speaks of the Father's attentive concern for people (Matt. 10:26–33 // Luke 12:4–12). While many things could be cited, we will focus on three major things in these passages about the Father and his ways toward people.

First, the Father compassionately and unconditionally loves all people. The first place in the narratives of both Matthew and Luke where Jesus speaks in some detail about the Father is the command to love one's enemies (Matt. 5:43–48 // Luke 6:27–36). While we are accustomed to thinking of love as an emotion, Jesus teaches that love is primarily an action. The parallelism of Jesus's words indicates that "Love your enemies" means the same thing as "Do good to those who hate you" (Luke 6:27). Moreover, Jesus's framing of the love command in terms of love for enemies underscores that genuine love is not self-centered or self-serving. Since an enemy shows hate and not love, to love one's enemies means that one should do good to all without expecting anything in return. When Jesus says that we should love our enemies, it means (among other things) that we should do good to others irrespective of whether they will do good to us in return. The reason why Jesus commands us to love in this way is because this is how the Father treats us. The Father loves those who love him and loves those who hate him. Jesus makes this clear by saying that the Father "makes his sun rise on the evil and on the good, and sends rain on the righteous and on the unrighteous" (Matt. 5:45). And in Luke, Jesus states that the Most High is "good to the ungrateful and the wicked" (Luke 6:35, my translation). Furthermore, Jesus says that those who practice this manner of genuine love will be "children [lit., sons] of your Father in heaven" (Matt. 5:45; cf. Luke 6:35).[42] Recall that in the biblical tradition, an ideal son is one who learns from and imitates the ways of his father. Therefore, to be "sons" of the "Father in heaven" means to follow the Father's example that Jesus himself, as *the* Son of the Father, shows us.[43] Jesus displays such love on the cross when he prays for and forgives those who put him to death: "Father, forgive them; for they do not know what they are doing" (Luke 23:34).

While love is primarily the action of doing good to others without self-interest, it does involve dispositions of compassion and kindness. Jesus himself speaks of the Father in just this way. For instance, in the final line in Luke's account of the love command, Jesus says, "Be merciful, just as your Father is merciful" (6:36). The Greek word translated here as "merciful" is *oiktirmōn*. While the Father is very merciful in forgiving sins, the sense of this word in this context is more along the lines of "compassion" (cf. 2 Cor. 1:3; Phil 2:1; Col. 3:12). This teaching about the Father's compassion alludes to Psalm 103:13 (102:13 LXX): "As a father has compassion [LXX: *oiktirei*]

42. Luke has "children [lit., sons] of the Most High" (6:35).
43. In Luke 1:32, the angel Gabriel says that Jesus "will be called Son of the Most High," and in Luke 6:35, Jesus teaches that those who love in this manner "will be sons of the Most High" (translation mine).

for his children, so the LORD has compassion [LXX: *oiktirēsen*] for those who fear him." The Father is compassionate to people, and Jesus instructs his disciples to do the same.

Second, the Father intimately knows and cares for people, all of whom are precious in his eyes. Matthew and Luke provide a unit of teaching in which Jesus tells his disciples about the Father's loving providence (Matt. 6:25–34 // Luke 12:22–32). The Father is the Creator of all things (Matt. 19:4), and Jesus invites us to see the Father's providence at work in the world: he enables the sun to rise and set and the rain to fall (Matt. 5:45); he provides for the birds and covers the fields with flowers (Luke 12:24, 27–28). Jesus then compares the Father's care for the birds and the flowers to his care for human beings. Using a Jewish mode of argumentation known as *qal vaḥomer* ("the light and the heavy"), Jesus teaches that the Father's care and concern for human beings far exceeds his care and concern for other created things. The logic of the argument runs like this: if the Father takes care of the birds and the flowers of the field, which are here today and gone tomorrow, then how much more will he take care of people: "Of how much more value are you than the birds!" (Luke 12:24). These sayings illustrate not only the Father's loving care but also the inestimable value that every human being has in his eyes.

The Father has a perfect, intimate knowledge of us all, including the tiny aspects of our lives ("even the hairs of your head are all counted"; Luke 12:7). Nothing is hidden from the Father's gaze, for he "sees in secret" (Matt. 6:4, 6, 18). Knowing perfectly every aspect of our existence, the Father knows all of our needs and generously provides what we need to live in a manner pleasing to him (6:31–34).[44] So intimate and perfect is the Father's knowledge that Jesus says, "Your Father knows what you need before you ask him" (6:8). Jesus points out that human fathers (all of whom are sinners) know to some extent what it is to give good things to their children. If sinful human beings have some inkling of what giving a good thing is, then imagine how much more generous with good is the heavenly Father,

44. See chap. 4 below.

who is perfect (5:48). As Jesus teaches, "If you then, who are evil, know how to give good gifts to your children, how much more will your Father in heaven give good things to those who ask him" (7:11). Jesus invites people to trust the Father and to depend on him with confidence. Such teaching appears in a unit where Jesus talks about the need to have confidence in times of trouble (Matt. 10:26–33 // Luke 12:2–9). Jesus tells his disciples that they will meet persecution and find themselves in difficult situations (Matt. 10:16–23; Luke 12:4–7). While the Father may not spare Jesus's disciples these trials, he will be present to them in the midst of these trials. In such times, Jesus says, the Father will provide the Holy Spirit to his disciples, who will enable them to bear witness to Jesus and the Father (Matt. 10:18–20, 32–33). The Father loves and provides for his people in all situations, and Jesus encourages people to have trust and confidence in the Father's goodness.

Third, the Father wants to form people and their conduct to be like him. The Father loves all people unconditionally and compassionately. But he is not content to leave people in their sins, living lives that offend him. Accordingly, Jesus teaches his disciples to put into practice certain attitudes and behaviors that reflect the Father himself. For, as Jesus says, "Not everyone who says to me, 'Lord, Lord,' will enter the kingdom of heaven, but only the one who does the will of my Father in heaven" (Matt. 7:21).

Some of these teachings appear in places where Jesus speaks of people living as "sons" (or children) of the Father. Since in the biblical tradition a child learns from and obeys the Father, when Jesus speaks of people who perform certain actions as being children of the Father, he implies that the actions in question reflect the Father's. We have already seen that such behavior includes doing good and showing compassion to all selflessly (i.e., love of enemies). In Matthew's list of the Beatitudes, Jesus says, "Blessed are the peacemakers, for they will be called children [lit., sons] of God" (Matt. 5:9). The statement implies that "peacemaking" (i.e., work for reconciliation and well-being) is God's work, a claim that is found in the Scriptures and other

Jewish texts (e.g., Isa. 45:7; Jer. 33:6, 9 [40:6, 9 LXX]; 2 Macc. 1:4; 3 Macc. 2:20). Those who similarly work for peace, reconciliation, and well-being imitate the Father as his children.

Jesus's Father Becomes "Our Father"

Jesus has a unique relationship with the Father as the Son. But he does not keep this relationship all to himself. Rather, Jesus opens up his relationship with the Father and incorporates his disciples into it. By sharing in Jesus's own relationship with the Father as the Son, Jesus's disciples can, therefore, call God "Father" and relate to him as his children. This obtains in one way during Jesus's public ministry and in another, even more profound and powerful way after his death and resurrection.

The Situation during Jesus's Public Ministry

Focusing on Matthew and Luke, we see cases during his public ministry where Jesus speaks of incorporating his disciples into his relationship with the Father. First, Matthew and Luke present Jesus using the expression "your Father" when he speaks to his disciples and sympathetic crowds. In both Gospels, Jesus speaks of God as "my Father" and himself as the Son, and he also tells his disciples that God is "your Father." On one level, to call God "Father" or think of him as the Father of a group or an individual is an established element in biblical tradition and piety. Yet, interestingly, Jesus uses the phrase "your Father" only when he is speaking to his disciples or those open to becoming his disciples. In Matthew, Jesus uses the phrase "your Father" most extensively in the Sermon on the Mount, which is spoken primarily to his disciples and by extension to the sympathetic crowds (4:25–5:2; 7:28).[45] All other uses of "your Father" in Matthew are spoken to Jesus's disciples (10:20; 18:14; 23:9). In

45. See Matt. 5:16, 45, 48; 6:1, 4, 6, 8, 14–15, 18, 26, 32; 7:11. On the crowds in Matthew, see Kingsbury, *Matthew as Story*, 24–25.

Luke, Jesus uses the phrase less frequently, but here too, he says it only to his disciples (6:36; 12:30, 32). By reserving the phrase "your Father" for Jesus's disciples and those en route to becoming disciples, Matthew and Luke invite us to see that the relationship with the Father of which Jesus speaks is distinctive. Only Jesus makes this sort of relationship with the Father possible for people, and they enter into this relationship with the Father through their positive response to Jesus himself.

A second example is the scene, given in all three Synoptics, where Jesus talks about his family members (Matt. 12:46–50 // Mark 3:31–35 // Luke 8:19–21). The three Synoptic accounts present the same core elements. While Jesus is teaching, his mother and brothers arrive and want to speak with him. But they are unable to reach Jesus on account of a group separating them from him. When Jesus hears that his family members have arrived, he makes a statement as to who makes up his family and does so with reference to those who have come to hear him.

Each evangelist locates this episode in a different part of his Gospel narrative, and each, through differences in context and wording, draws out different dimensions of its significance. Matthew presents the words of Jesus in this way: "Jesus replied, 'Who is my mother, and who are my brothers?' And pointing to his disciples, he said, 'Here are my mother and my brothers! For whoever does the will of my Father in heaven is my brother and sister and mother'" (12:48–50). Matthew explicitly says that Jesus speaks these words with reference to his "disciples" (12:49). His family members are those who do "the will of my Father in heaven" (12:50). As the Son, not only does Jesus make known the Father's will (11:27), but he himself also does the Father's will perfectly. This is especially on display in the Gospel's passion narrative: "My Father, if this cannot pass unless I drink it, your will be done" (26:42).

For his part, Luke locates the family episode in a narrative sequence with the parable of the sower (8:4–8, 11–15). Luke's version of the parable of the sower has a strong emphasis on the need to take in and embrace the word Jesus speaks (i.e., the "seed") in order for it to produce mature fruit (8:4–8, 11–15).[46] After some related teaching about the need to listen (8:16–18), Luke gives us the episode of Jesus and his family (8:19–21). Luke presents this episode in terms that recall the parable of the sower. The terrains in the parable are different modes in which people "hear" Jesus's word. The good soil is a mode of taking in Jesus's word wherein those "who, when they hear the word, hold it fast in an honest and good heart, and bear fruit with patient endurance" (8:15). In the family scene, when Jesus speaks of his mother and brothers, he does so in terms that recall the "good soil" (8:8) in the parable: "My mother and my brothers are those who hear the word of God and do it" (8:21). Jesus's kin are those who receive the word he teaches and then put it into practice—that is, they are Jesus's disciples.

Jesus and his disciples form a family, a kinship group, and this family has Jesus's Father for their Father. By becoming Jesus's disciples through faith and discipleship, people become his kin and share in his relationship with the Father. Jesus's Father thus becomes the Father of the disciples who have attached themselves to Jesus. As the Son, Jesus does the Father's will completely, and those who receive Jesus's word about the Father and follow his ways can also be called the Father's children.

The Situation after the Resurrection

After Jesus's death and resurrection, an even more intimate, profound, and powerful relationship with the Father becomes possible for Jesus's disciples. This post-resurrection context is important because it is the one from which Christians in all times and places offer the Lord's Prayer to the Father.

For our purposes, we will examine two important passages from Saint Paul that speak to this post-resurrection relationship with the Father. In Romans 8:12–17 and Galatians 4:1–7, Paul speaks of Chris-

---

46. See Wright and Martin, *Encountering the Living God*, 232–36.

tians being adopted by God the Father and thus becoming his children through their relationship to the risen Jesus and by the action of the Holy Spirit.

Galatians 4:1–7 fits within Paul's larger argument about how God's promise of blessing and righteousness is fulfilled and made available to gentiles through Jesus (3:1–4:31).[47] He teaches that through faith and baptism, Christians have become "sons of God" (*huioi theou*; 3:26, my translation). They are spiritually united to Christ through baptism and are thus beneficiaries of God's promises to Abraham (3:27–29). As a result of Christ's redemptive action, the baptized receive from God the gift of "adoption as children" (4:5). Christians become God's "sons" (*huioi*; 3:26) by sharing in the life and reality of God's "Son" (*huios*; 4:4). This is what divine adoption means: God becomes our Father because through baptism we are spiritually united to the risen Jesus and share in his own relationship with the Father.

Integral to this new relationship is the interior presence and action of the Holy Spirit.[48] Through baptism into Christ, the Holy Spirit comes to indwell Christians (cf. Gal. 3:27–29). Paul writes, "Because you are sons [*huioi*], God has sent the Spirit of his Son into our hearts, crying, 'Abba! Father!'" (4:6 alt.).[49] As Francis Martin puts it, "By the action of the Holy Spirit, Christians now know a share in the relation that Jesus had and has with the Father."[50] That is, through their union with the Son, which is brought about and known by the Holy Spirit, Christians can relate to and address God as Jesus does: "Abba! Father!" (4:6).

Paul gives a similar picture in Romans 8:12–17. In Romans 8, Paul teaches about the gift of the Holy Spirit and the new state of life (freedom from sin's spiritual oppression) that the Spirit brings about

47. On the structuring of Galatians and 3:1–4:31 in particular, see Betz, *Galatians*, 14–23, 128–30.
48. I am indebted to Francis Martin on this topic.
49. NRSV translation emended to show the lexical connection between Jesus's identity as "the Son" (*huios*) and the identity of Christians as "sons" (*huioi*).
50. Martin, *Feminist Question*, 282.

in Christians. The Spirit, Paul specifies, is the Spirit of God the Father and Jesus Christ, and the Spirit comes to indwell the baptized (8:10–11). The indwelling Holy Spirit is the powerful source of life in whom Christians live in the present time, in the end-time resurrection, and into eternity.

As in Galatians 4, Paul talks about the action of the Holy Spirit in Christians becoming adopted children of the Father. He writes, "All who are led by the Spirit of God are children [lit., sons; *huioi*] of God" (Rom. 8:14). Paul later adds, "You received a Spirit of adoption by whom we cry out 'Abba! Father!'" (8:15, my translation). The Holy Spirit makes us to be the Father's adopted children as we share in the life and reality of Jesus the Son (8:15).

The Spirit, moreover, works in people a knowledge and awareness that they are the Father's adopted children: "It is that very Spirit bearing witness with our spirit that we are children of God" (Rom. 8:16). Martin writes the following about the spiritual dimensions of Paul's teaching here: Paul "tells us that the work of the Holy Spirit is to create within our hearts a divine affection for God the Father. Thus, responding to the revelation of God the Father to our consciousness, we can freely say to him, 'Abba,' Father."[51] The Spirit gives to Christians a deep, soul-touching awareness that we have been adopted by God the Father. This gift of illumination from the Spirit involves coming to know and experience the Father's love in a new way, for we can now relate to the Father as Jesus relates to the Father. As a result, Christians can address the Father as Jesus does: "We cry, 'Abba! Father!'" (8:15).

Christians today are in the same situation as Christians of the first century: we live after the death and resurrection of Jesus and have access to the relationship with the Father made possible by these events. Those spiritual realities described by Paul, of becoming the Father's adopted children and relating to him as Abba, apply to us today as well. And so, as we bring all these observations to bear on the opening address of the Lord's Prayer, we need to think of the

---

51. Martin, *Life-Changer*, 19.

words "our Father" in terms of the relationship with the Father that the risen Jesus makes possible for his disciples in all times and places, a relationship brought about and energized by the Holy Spirit.

Our Father in Heaven

Having examined Jesus's teachings about the Father and his relationship with the Father, which he shares with his disciples, we bring these observations to bear on the opening address of the Lord's Prayer.

First, when Christians pray "our Father," we pray in spiritual communion with Jesus, through whom we know and relate to the Father. Christians know and address God the Father (in doctrinal terms, the First Person of the Trinity) primarily through Jesus. In the Old Testament, God is known and addressed as "Father" on the basis of his relation to created individuals and groups. Thus, God is the Father of the people Israel, the Davidic king, and the righteous or wise person. This relation is constituted by God's gracious act of choosing people or by people imitating his ways. In the New Testament, the fatherhood of God is revealed to be constituted primarily by his relation to Jesus the Son. Put in doctrinal terms, the Father is the Father by virtue of his relation to the Son. As the divine Son, Jesus enjoys a unique relationship of familial closeness with the Father. Conceived by the Holy Spirit, Jesus is the Son by generation, not adoption. Jesus alone knows the Father as his Son, and as such, Jesus is able to reveal the Father in a unique, unparalleled way. Moreover, as the Son, Jesus perfectly and completely obeys the Father's will, and accordingly, in his human words and deeds, Jesus displays the Father and his ways to people.

Matthew's version of the Lord's Prayer has the modifier "in heaven" (Matt. 6:9) when speaking of the Father. Jonathan Pennington has shown that Matthew often uses the language of "heaven" to underscore the transcendence of God and his kingdom in contrast to things of "earth."[52] The modifier "in heaven" emphasizes the Father's

---

52. Pennington, *Heaven and Earth*, chap. 10, esp. 247–51.

otherness and distinction from the world. And yet, we come to know and relate to the heavenly Father through Jesus the Son (11:27).

Christians come into relationship with Jesus, and by entering into relationship with Jesus, we enter into his own relationship with the Father. During his public ministry, Jesus speaks of his disciples as his family members. The basis of Jesus's kinship group is doing the Father's will, which he makes known. Jesus's disciples become God's children (and thus Jesus's kin) by learning from and obeying the Father, whose ways are revealed and lived by Jesus the Son. Even more profound is the spiritual union of life with the risen Jesus, made possible after his resurrection and the sending of the Holy Spirit. Paul speaks of the Holy Spirit, the Spirit of God's Son, being poured into the baptized. The Spirit brings about a real, spiritual union with Christ the Son, and accordingly, the baptized become God's adopted children (or "sons") by participating in the life of *the* Son. By sharing in the life of the Son, the baptized also share in his relationship with the Father. Hence, the Spirit moves within the baptized and enables them to address the Father as Jesus does: "God has sent the Spirit of his Son into our hearts, crying, 'Abba! Father!'" (Gal. 4:6).

When Christians address God as "Father" in prayer, we address him within our spiritual relationship with Jesus, his Son and our brother. He is "our Father" because we share in the life and the reality of Jesus, his Son.

Second, when Christians pray "our Father," we pray in communion with other Christians as members of Christ's church. Jesus speaks of his community of disciples as a kinship group, a family with God as its Father. We become members of this family by following Jesus with faith and discipleship and becoming spiritually united to him through baptism and the Holy Spirit. As we enter into communion with Jesus (and through him with the Father), so also do we enter into communion with each other as members of the church. Seen in this way, the Lord's Prayer is an ecclesial prayer, a prayer shared and offered by all of Christ's followers and spiritual siblings.

The ecclesial character of the Lord's Prayer is underscored by the locations in Matthew and Luke where Jesus teaches the prayer. Both Matthew and Luke present the Lord's Prayer as being taught to the disciples as a group. In Luke, a disciple asks Jesus on behalf of the group, "Lord, teach *us* to pray" (11:1, emphasis added). Jesus responds by teaching the prayer to the group as a whole: "When you [plural] pray . . ." (11:2). Matthew places the Lord's Prayer in the Sermon on the Mount, a discourse addressed primarily to Jesus's disciples and then to the sympathetic crowds (4:25–5:2). Throughout the sermon, Jesus speaks to his audience of God as "your Father," with the "your" always in the plural. Similarly, he teaches them to address God in prayer as members of this group: "*Our* Father" (emphasis added).

The language of the prayer also reveals its communal character. In both Matthew's version and Luke's version of the prayer, everything pertaining to the Father and his actions is always given in the singular (i.e., the "your" that modifies the Father's "name," "kingdom," and "will" is singular). But everything pertaining to human beings in the Lord's Prayer is always given in the plural (e.g., repeated uses of "us" and "our"). The words of the prayer point to a communal, or church, setting for this prayer. Even when an individual Christian says this prayer, he or she says it as part of the larger community of believers.

The ecclesial aspect of the Lord's Prayer should lead Christians to recognize that all baptized disciples of Jesus (even those belonging to different ecclesial traditions) are brothers and sisters in Christ. While there do exist today real church-dividing differences between Christian communities, there are also real relationships and connections between all believers united to Christ. Through baptism, all believers come to share in the one life of the risen Jesus and relate to the Father through him. When, therefore, Christians say "our Father," we implicitly affirm our relation to fellow believers as brothers and sisters in Christ. We are all brothers and sisters because we all have the same Father through the Son.

Third, by giving us this prayer, Jesus invites us to know the Father's goodness and come to imitate his ways. The Lord's Prayer is a series of petitions, and it sits within the larger body of Jesus's teaching about the Father. By giving us this prayer, Jesus teaches us that the Father wants us to make requests of him. As in the parable of the persistent neighbor (Luke 11:5–8), the Father wants us to knock always on his door with our prayers, and for his part, the Father is eager to give us the good things that we need. The Father wants and does what is good for all people—that is, the Father loves each one of us unconditionally. This series of petitions shows us that the Father is good and generous.

With these petitions, Jesus teaches us what we really need and what we should ask for from the Father. For one, these petitions illustrate Jesus's point about the Father's intimate and perfect knowledge of each of us ("Your Father knows what you need before you ask him"; Matt. 6:8). At the same time, these petitions also instruct us about who we are and what it is that we are really in need of. To reiterate the words of Augustine about the Lord's Prayer: "The words our Lord Jesus Christ has taught us in his prayer give us the framework of true desires."[53] C. Clifton Black makes a similar claim about the Lord's Prayer: "The Prayer reforms our manifold 'wanting' as human creatures. What we most profoundly *need* is evoked and exposed. What we most ardently *desire* is developed and disciplined."[54] By giving us this prayer, Jesus is revealing not only the Father but also things about us to ourselves.[55] The petitions in the Lord's Prayer show us who we are and what we need to ask for from God.

■ Conclusion

Jesus's teaching about the Father is a distinctive part of his ministry. "Father" was a known name for God in the Scriptures and in Jewish

53. Augustine, *Essential Sermons*, 56.5 (Hill, 86).
54. Black, *Lord's Prayer*, xxi.
55. Cf. the famous statement of the Second Vatican Council in *Gaudium et Spes* (no. 22): "Only in the mystery of the incarnate Word does the mystery of man take on light. For Adam, the first man, was a figure of Him Who was to come, namely Christ the Lord. Christ, the final Adam, by the revelation of the mystery of the Father and His love, fully reveals man to man himself and makes his supreme calling clear."

piety, and Jesus reveals it as the central name for God. Both Matthew and Luke teach that Jesus is the divine Son of God from the moment of his conception. During his ministry, Jesus teaches that he has a unique relationship with the Father as the Son, a status that distinguishes him from the prophets of Israel. As the Son, Jesus is able to reveal the Father and his ways in a unique and unparalleled way. In his public ministry, Jesus displays his divine Sonship not only by revealing the Father but also by his life of total love and obedience toward the Father. Through his human life of perfect faithfulness and obedience, Jesus lives out the vocation of Israel as God's covenant people, his "firstborn son" (Exod. 4:22). Jesus also opens up his relationship with the Father to his disciples. This obtains in one mode during his public ministry and in a different mode after Jesus's death and resurrection. For after his death and resurrection, the risen Jesus offers to all people a share in his own life through baptism and the Holy Spirit. By entering into communion of life with the risen Jesus, the baptized also enter into communion with his Father and thus relate to him as such.

When Christians pray "our Father," we pray within the spiritual communion with the Father that we have through our communion with Jesus his Son. The baptized are children of the Father because we share in the life of the Father's Son Jesus. The communion of spiritual life with Jesus entails that the baptized exist in communion with each other. This is the spiritual reality of the church. Thus, the Lord's Prayer is an ecclesial prayer. It is the prayer of Jesus's disciples and adopted siblings, who all have the same Father. By praying the Lord's Prayer, we address and relate to our heavenly Father, who teaches us not only about himself but also about who we are and what we truly need. Through the petitions of the Lord's Prayer, Jesus invites us to know the love and goodness of the Father, who will "give good things to those who ask him" (Matt. 7:11).

3

Sanctify Your Name

After teaching us to call on the Father by name, Jesus gives us the first group of petitions in the Lord's Prayer, the "you" petitions. As mentioned in chapter 1, these petitions are so called because they all center on something of the Father's (e.g., his name, kingdom, and will) and contain the adjective "your" (singular).

The first petition that Jesus teaches us to ask the Father is "hallowed be your name" (Matt. 6:9 // Luke 11:2). To hallow means to sanctify or to make holy. At once, the language of this petition raises a number of questions: What does it mean to make the Father's name holy? Isn't his name holy to begin with? And who does the sanctifying? Is it the Father or human beings or both? How can sinful, finite people make the Father's name holy when he is already the "Holy One of Israel" (Ps. 71:22)?

During his ministry, Jesus says much about other topics mentioned in the Lord's Prayer, such as the kingdom of God and forgiveness. But he does not talk about sanctifying the Father's name outside of the Lord's Prayer. Accordingly, to gain insight into this petition, we will have to rely more on the scriptural allusions this petition contains, for the two principal elements in this petition—God's "name" and the verb "to sanctify" (Hb. *qādaš*; Gk. *hagiazō*)—both have a rich theological significance in the Scriptures.

Taken in light of its biblical allusions, *the name petition is a request for the Father to manifest his holiness by bringing his saving plan to its full completion with the result that people will rightly praise and honor him.*

▨ The Language of the Petition

The wording of the name petition is the same in Matthew and Luke: *hagiasthētō to onoma sou.* The Greek phrase *to onoma sou* straightforwardly means "your name." The phrase "hallowed be" is the conventional English translation of the verb *hagiasthētō.* Grammatically, *hagiasthētō* is an imperative form (i.e., a command) of the verb *hagiazō*, which means "to sanctify" or "to make holy." This imperative has "your name" for its subject, and it is in the passive voice. The language of the petition can thus be translated more literally as "Your name be sanctified."

Two other features of Greek syntax illumine this petition. First, the use of the passive voice here is known as the "divine passive." It is a Semitic way of speaking that employs the passive voice in order to avoid directly using the word "God";[1] that is, it is a way of referring to God or claiming that God acts without actually having to use the word "God." The use of the divine passive in the command "be sanctified" implies that the Father is the primary actor. In this petition, we primarily ask the Father to sanctify his name. Second, the verb *hagiasthētō* is an imperative in the aorist tense. As mentioned in chapter 1, an imperative in the aorist tense is customarily understood as asking for an action to be done on a single occasion.[2] So understood, the petition asks the Father to sanctify his name, and it looks for this action to be completed at one time.

1. Jeremias, *New Testament Theology*, 9–14.
2. Cf. Béchard, *Syntax of New Testament*, §3.1 (pp. 37–39).

Your "Name"

There is a significant line of thought in many biblical texts (and the ancient world more generally) that considers a person's name to be more than just a term of address.[3] A person's name articulated his or her identity and role in the world. This association between name and identity appears in biblical texts where God gives a person a new name. The new name often has a meaning that corresponds to that person's new role in God's plan. For instance, in Genesis 17, God changes Abram's name to Abraham in connection with the promise that he will be "the [father] of a multitude of nations [Hb. *'ab-hămôn gôyim*]" (v. 5). The name Abraham (Hb. *'abrāhām*) reflects the Hebrew words for "father" (*'āb*) and "multitude" (*hāmôn*). Accordingly, this man's identity is henceforth bound up with God's promise to make him the ancestor of a great many people. When God changes Abram's name, he, in a sense, changes *who* Abram *is* and gives him a new, distinctive role in the divine economy.

This same connection between a person's name and his or her identity holds true, analogously, with respect to God. When God appears to Moses in the burning bush, Moses asks God for his name, and God replies, "I am whom I am" (Exod. 3:14). This phrase is etymologically linked to the name YHWH—both are grounded in the Hebrew verb *hāyâ* ("to be"). Without delving into how to interpret the meaning of God's sacred name in Exodus 3, we can say for present purposes that the revelation of God's sacred name is a profound and mysterious revelation of who God is.[4]

The close relationship between God's self and his name also appears in texts that associate God's name and the Jerusalem temple. The Jerusalem temple is the place where the radically transcendent God comes to dwell among his people in a special way. To affirm both God's transcendent difference from the world and his immanent

---

3. Eichrodt, *Theology of the Old Testament*, 2:40–45.
4. In some biblical texts, God's "name" also has the sense of being God's reputation. This often appears where God acts, and as a result his fame or renown increases in the world. See Exod. 9:16; 14:4; Neh. 9:10; Pss. 25:11; 79:9; Ezek. 36:23; Dan. 9:19.

presence to it, Deuteronomy often speaks of the Jerusalem temple as the place where God's "name" dwells, rather than simply God himself—as if God's name was quasi-distinct from God himself.[5] Thus, Deuteronomy 12 speaks of the temple as "the place that the LORD your God will choose as a dwelling for his name" (v. 11). At the dedication of the Jerusalem temple, King Solomon quotes the Lord's own declaration about the temple, "My name shall be there" (1 Kings 8:29). Such texts speak of God's "name" as dwelling in the temple so as to maintain the transcendent otherness of God while also affirming that God has genuinely come near to his people Israel and dwells among them.

In the New Testament, the God of Israel comes to dwell among people in an even more profound and heretofore unimaginable manner: he becomes human in Jesus of Nazareth. As God become human without any loss of his divinity, Jesus reveals the identity of the God of Israel in a more intimate and intensive way.[6] He reveals God with the name "Father" and himself as the Father's "Son." Jesus further reveals that the identity of God includes the Holy Spirit when he gives his disciples the mandate to baptize "in the name of the Father and of the Son and of the Holy Spirit" (Matt. 28:19).[7] Not only do these words provide the form for Christian baptism, but they also point to baptism as the introduction of the baptized into the very life of God. That is, with this trinitarian formula, Christians are baptized into the "name"—that is, the reality of the blessed Trinity—and come to share in the divine life.

More immediate to the Lord's Prayer, however, is the name "Father." The prayer is, after all, addressed to the Father. When the petition speaks of "your name," the personal adjective "your" modifies

5. Von Rad, *Studies in Deuteronomy*, 37–39.

6. Robert Sokolowski (*Eucharistic Presence*, 54) writes, "There is also an intensification between the Jewish and the New Testament understandings of God. There is a difference even though there is not an otherness. . . . The God who is called 'Father' by Christ is the same God who spoke to Moses and spoke through the prophets, but he is more deeply revealed to us when he is so addressed by Jesus."

7. The framing of things in terms of the "identity of God" is indebted to Bauckham, *Jesus and the God of Israel*.

"Father." The name the petition asks to be sanctified is the name "Father." Given the association between a person's name and identity, the petition asks that not only the Father's name but also the Father himself be sanctified.

Sanctification and Holiness

The verb in the name petition for "hallowed be" or "sanctify" (*hagiazō*) fits within the larger biblical teaching on holiness. Throughout the Bible, a preeminent attribute of God is holiness, and God is often pronounced to be holy in liturgical settings. In the call vision of Isaiah, the prophet is given to see angelic seraphim around God's throne, singing, "Holy, holy, holy is the LORD of hosts" (Isa. 6:3; cf. Rev. 4:8). The book of Revelation recalls Isaiah when John sees the heavenly worship of God, led by the four angelic creatures who continually sing, "Holy, holy, holy, the Lord God the Almighty, who was and is and is to come" (Rev. 4:8).

Ingredient to the biblical notion of holiness is the idea of difference. The biblical tradition sets forth a particular understanding of God as being distinct from the world; the Creator is not part of the creation, nor does he depend on creation in any way.[8] God's otherness to the world informs the biblical notion of holiness. As God is distinct from the world and perfectly holy, so holiness involves being different or set apart from things of the world.

God is the Creator and Lord of all, and all peoples and things belong to him (Exod. 19:5; Ps. 24:1). God can also bring things (or permit things to be brought) into a special kind of relationship with him. The bringing of worldly things or people into just such a relationship with God and for his purposes is "sanctification." When people and things are brought into this special contact with God, "the Holy One of Israel" (Isa. 12:6), they acquire "holiness" as a quality.

8. This point has been expertly and thematically explored by Sokolowski in his theological writings. For a foundational account of the distinction between God and the world, see his *God of Faith and Reason*.

What is holy, therefore, exists in a special relationship with God and becomes, in a sense, different from other things in the world.

These themes appear in the election and covenant with Israel at Mount Sinai. When God offers a covenant relationship to the people Israel at Mount Sinai, he says to them, "You shall be my treasured possession out of all the peoples. Indeed, the whole earth is mine, but you shall be for me a priestly kingdom and a holy nation" (Exod. 19:5–6). While all peoples in the world belong to God, he is choosing the people Israel to be in a special covenant relationship with him, and in their distinctive status, they will be a "holy nation"—that is, they will be a people set apart from other nations. By living according to God's Torah, the people Israel show forth the ways of the Lord and his holiness: "You shall be holy, for I the Lord your God am holy" (Lev. 19:2).[9]

The biblical notions of sanctification and holiness are very important in Israel's worship of God. Their liturgical life presupposes a distinction between the holy and the worldly.[10] That is, in biblical thinking, there is a kind of spiritual quality or space that things pertaining to God partake of in a special way. This quality or space is "holiness." Various people and things in Israel's liturgical life are consecrated to God and are thus holy; they are "set apart" from worldly things for God and his service. Things that are not especially dedicated to God exist in the domain of the worldly. The domain of the worldly is not bad. Rather, it is the common state of things that are not especially given over to God for his service.

Sanctified people and things continue to exist in the world in which sin and impurity (or "uncleanness") also exist. Accordingly, it is possible for holy people and things to become contaminated or tainted by what is impure. The Scriptures state that certain actions "profane" or "defile" what is holy. Jonathan Klawans explains that there are two

9. Luke Johnson (*Writings of the New Testament*, 40) puts it well: "By observing [the commandments], Israel was to show all peoples that God is holy, that is, utterly different from any imaginable powers on earth. Israel was to be a 'holy nation' (Exod. 19:6), different from other peoples on the earth."

10. See Nelson, *Raising Up a Faithful Priest*, 17–38.

principal kinds of impurity in the Scriptures.[11] First, there is "ritual impurity," which means that a person is not in a proper state to be near the divine presence or participate in liturgical rites. Ritual impurity is not necessarily sinful, and a person could become ritually impure through a variety of natural processes or good actions. Being purified from most ritual impurities was usually straightforward, often requiring only washing and waiting for a designated time. But if something ritually impure was to come into contact with something holy, the latter would be defiled or polluted (e.g., Lev. 15:31). Second, there is also "moral impurity," which is caused by serious sins like idolatry, sexual sin, and murder.[12] The Scriptures refer to these serious sins as an "abomination" (Hb. *tôʿēbâ*; LXX: *bdelygma*), and as Klawans writes, these sins "bring about an impurity that *morally*—but not *ritually*—defiles the sinner (Lev. 18:24), the land of Israel (Lev. 18:25; Ezek. 36:17), and the sanctuary of God (Lev. 20:3; Ezek. 5:11)."[13]

In the Torah, God provided Israel with liturgical rites to decontaminate sacred things and restore to a state of proper holiness that which had been profaned (Lev. 16:16). Yet, the people's serious sins and their resulting moral impurity could accumulate to the point where the special presence of God among his people was itself put in jeopardy. God would become so "fed up" with his people's sins that he would withdraw his special presence among his people and leave the temple (Jer. 7:5–7; Ezek. 10). Klawans writes, "God finds [these sins] so abhorrent that He will not and cannot abide on a land that becomes saturated with the residue left by their performance."[14]

That is what the biblical writers present as having happened at the end of the monarchy in ancient Israel (2 Kings 17:7–18; 21:10–15; 24:1–4; 25). As punishment for sins, God enacted the consequences for disobedience that the covenant stipulated: exile and scattering. This punishment came by way of the people's enemies, who

---

11. Klawans, *Purity, Sacrifice, and the Temple*, esp. 53–56.
12. Klawans, *Purity, Sacrifice, and the Temple*, 55.
13. Klawans, *Purity, Sacrifice, and the Temple*, 55.
14. Klawans, *Purity, Sacrifice, and the Temple*, 70.

conquered them and took them into exile: the Assyrian conquest of the ten northern tribes of Israel in 722/721 BC and the Babylonian conquest of the two southern tribes of Judah in 587 BC.

Exposition of the Name Petition

The "name" of God and the action of "sanctifying" are both prominent topics in the Scriptures. But there are only a few places in Scripture where God's "name" is combined with the verb for "sanctifying." Given that Jesus does not talk about sanctifying the Father's name outside of the Lord's Prayer and that this is an infrequent combination of terms in the Scriptures, it is quite likely that these biblical texts are in view when Jesus gives us the name petition.

Sanctifying God's Name in the Old Testament

As God himself is supremely and perfectly holy, so too do many biblical texts declare that God's name is "holy."[15] In Leviticus, the Lord declares, "I the LORD your God am holy" (19:2) and elsewhere speaks of his "holy name" (20:3; 22:2, 32). Various religious practices are likewise associated with God's name. Priests in ancient Israel would bless in the Lord's name (Num. 6:22–27; cf. Deut. 10:8; 21:5), and a true prophet speaks in the Lord's name (Deut. 18:19). The psalms also summon Israelites to worship God by performing a variety of actions with respect to God's name. These include, for example, declarations to "sing praise to the name of the LORD" (Ps. 7:17); to "bless his holy name" (103:1); to "praise your name" (145:2); to "glorify your name" (86:9); and to "call on the name of the LORD" (116:13).

While Scripture prescribes many different actions to be performed with respect to God's name, they do not often feature the specific

---

15. Lev. 20:3; 22:2, 32; 1 Chron. 16:10, 35; 29:16; Pss. 33:21; 105:3; 106:47; 111:9; 145:21; Ezek. 20:39; 36:20–22; 39:7, 25; 43:7–8; Dan. 3:52; Amos 2:7. So too Tob. 3:11; 13:11, 18; 2 Macc. 8:15; Wis. 10:20; Sir. 17:10; 23:9–10.

association given in the Lord's Prayer: to sanctify the name of God. There are a few significant passages in the Scriptures where God's "name" and "sanctifying" are combined, and these passages shed light on the name petition: Leviticus 22:32; Ezekiel 36:23; Isaiah 29:23. Of these three, Ezekiel 36:23 and Isaiah 29:23 are the most pertinent for the name petition.

As we will see, since God and his name are perfectly holy in themselves, sanctifying God's name does not mean making God's name holy (as if it was not holy to begin with) or making God's holiness greater in some way (how can we add to God's perfection?). Instead, it is more helpful to think of sanctifying God's name in terms of *displaying God's holiness.*

Ezekiel 36:23

The prophet Ezekiel, who was also a priest, conducted his public ministry shortly before and then into the Babylonian exile. As a priest, Ezekiel often uses the language of sanctifying and profaning when delivering his prophetic message. He also speaks of God acting "for the sake of [his] name" (Ezek. 20:9, 14, 22; 36:22).

In a historical review of Israel's covenant relationship with God, Ezekiel talks about Israel's sinful conduct in terms of profanation and defilement (Ezek. 20). Through a history of idolatrous and seriously sinful conduct, the Israelites have morally defiled themselves (20:7, 18, 31). Through such serious sins, they have polluted themselves as God's chosen people and thus rendered themselves unfit for God's special presence. While God would be in the right to destroy his unfaithful people for their sins, he does not do so, "for the sake of [his] name, that it should not be profaned in the sight of the nations" (20:9; cf. 20:14, 22).[16] Nevertheless, the contamination of abominable sins has become so great that Ezekiel has a vision of God's presence ("the glory of the LORD") leaving the temple and Jerusalem (Ezek. 10).

16. God's "name" here primarily has the sense of God's reputation.

A similar way of articulating things appears in Ezekiel 36:23. As in Ezekiel 20, the Lord speaks of Israel's sins as actions that defile: "They defiled [the holy land] with their ways and their deeds; their conduct in my sight was like [a great] uncleanness" (36:17). As a just punishment for their sins, God allowed them to be conquered by foreign nations, who took them into exile and among whom they were "scattered" and "dispersed" (36:19–20). At the same time, his people's sins and his consequent action to send them into exile reflected badly on the God of Israel in the eyes of the gentile nations. Hence, God's holy name was profaned by the very presence of his people in exile (36:20).

Therefore, in order to restore the majesty of his name, which had been profaned by his people, God promises to perform a great, eschatological saving act to make things right and so reveal his holiness to all (Ezek. 36:23; 37:21–28). This end-time saving action is the restoration of Israel, which he will perform "for the sake of [his] holy name" (36:22). The eschatological restoration of Israel provides the setting for the declaration that God will sanctify his name: "I will *sanctify my* great *name*, which has been profaned among the nations, and which you have profaned among them; and the nations shall know that I am the LORD, says the LORD God, when through you I display my holiness before their eyes" (36:23, emphasis added). That is, the Lord will display his holiness to all by performing this gracious saving act for his people in the end-time.

Elsewhere, Ezekiel speaks of many things that will figure into God's end-time action whereby he sanctifies his name. Among other things, God says that he will do the following: regather his people from exile and return them to the promised land (Ezek. 36:24; cf. 37:22, 25), transform his redeemed people from within and put his Spirit within them in a new covenant (36:26–27), transform the promised land to be like a new garden of Eden, and multiply the population of restored Israel (36:35–38). And as Ezekiel saw the glory of the Lord leaving the temple before its destruction, so also does he see the glory returning to dwell with his people forever in a new eschatological temple (37:27; 43:1–9). In this eschatological state of affairs, the Lord will receive right worship (20:39–40). Through these actions, God will also "sanctify Israel" (37:28), and all peoples on earth will come to know and acknowledge the holiness of the Lord, the God of Israel (36:23; 38:23; 39:7, 28).

In short, Ezekiel teaches that God will sanctify his name by bringing about the eschatological restoration of Israel and transforming the world. God will thus reveal his own holiness and also sanctify his people Israel, making them apt to receive his permanent dwelling with them (Ezek. 37:27–28). Through this gracious, end-time action, God will show forth to all peoples his holiness (39:27).

Isaiah 29:23

Another text that speaks of God's name being sanctified is Isaiah 29:23: "When [Jacob] sees his children, the work of my hands, in his midst, they will sanctify my name; they will sanctify the Holy One of Jacob, and will stand in awe of the God of Israel." Thematically similar to Ezekiel 36:23, Isaiah 29:23 appears within a set of prophetic teachings concerning God's eschatological action and the resulting state of affairs (29:15–24). Isaiah 29 speaks of a future transformation of the world that God will bring about in the end-time. The text announces that "the deaf shall hear the words of a scroll, and out of their gloom and darkness the eyes of the blind shall see" (29:18; cf. 35:5). At that time, God will likewise secure justice and righteousness in the world. The "meek" and "the neediest people" will rejoice in the Lord, and the wicked will be no more (29:19–21).

A new movement begins at Isaiah 29:22. The text identifies the Lord as the one "who redeemed Abraham" and speaks about "the house of Jacob" (29:22). The mention of the Lord's action as the Redeemer in the past sets up the prophet's speaking of his action to redeem "the house of Jacob" in the future. The text declares that the Lord will take away the shame of Jacob, who will again see his children standing before him (29:22–23). It envisions the future restoration of Jacob's children, the people Israel, from the state of exile.

The text goes on to articulate the response of restored Israel to God's saving action: "They will sanctify my name" (Isa. 29:23). Whereas in Ezekiel 36, the eschatological sanctifying of God's name is something that God does by restoring Israel, in Isaiah 29:23, it is the children of Jacob, having been restored from exile, who sanctify God's name in the eschatological state of affairs. In this context, to sanctify God's name is akin to praising and blessing God. This idea that people sanctify God's name as an act of praise appears in other ancient Jewish texts.[17] Most notably, the Kaddish uses such language and locates this action in the eschatological age, brought about by God's end-time saving action: "May his great name be magnified and sanctified in the world that is to be created anew, when he will revive the dead and raise them up unto life eternal."[18]

The restored people of God, Isaiah 29 continues, will likewise be changed. Their minds, which had previously been in error, will be corrected and enlightened. Their wills, which had been obstinate, will be made receptive to and compliant with God's teaching (29:24). In this eschatological state of affairs, the people Israel will manifest God's holiness not only by their praise but also through their reverential obedience.

"Hallowed Be Your Name" in the Lord's Prayer

We can now bring these biblical insights to bear on the name petition. When we pray "Hallowed be your name," we are asking the Father *to manifest his holiness by bringing his saving plan to its full completion with the result that people will rightly praise and honor him.*

Several indications point to the name petition as having an eschatological tone. As an aorist imperative, the command "hallowed be" or "be sanctified" (*hagiasthētō*) can be taken as looking for a single action to be performed in the future. The use of the divine passive

---

17. Cf. 1 En. 61:11; 4 Ezra 7:60; 2 Bar. 63:10.
18. Heinemann and Petuchowski, *Literature of the Synagogue*, 84.

in the petition implies that the Father will be the principal agent who does the sanctifying action. Both of these elements square with the language and vision of Ezekiel 36:23: "I will sanctify my great name, which has been profaned among the nations, and which you have profaned among them; and the nations shall know that I am the LORD, says the Lord GOD, when through you I display my holiness before their eyes." This text speaks of God manifesting his holiness when he works his eschatological act of salvation and transforms the world. Moreover, Ezekiel 36:23 is *the* biblical text that presents God as the one who sanctifies his name. It is therefore likely that Jesus invites us to understand the name petition in light of Ezekiel 36:23 and its eschatological vision of salvation. The petition "hallowed be your name" asks the Father to do what Ezekiel talks about: *to manifest his holiness by bringing his saving plan to its full completion.*

Moving to the New Testament—and in keeping with how Jesus spoke about his own ministry and mission—Christians believe that God's definitive eschatological saving action has *already* occurred in the death and resurrection of Jesus. His death deals with the problem of sin, and his resurrection marks the arrival, in a genuine but not yet fully realized way, of the eschatological state of affairs. And so, in one sense, the holiness of the Father has been manifested in the death and resurrection of his Son Jesus (cf. John 12:27–28; 17:1, 4–5).

At the same time, there are aspects of God's eschatological action in Christ that are yet to be realized in all their fullness. There remains a future part of the Christian eschatological picture. These future aspects will be fully realized at Christ's parousia (more popularly known as the second coming of Christ). In the ancient world, the term "parousia" could refer to the official visit of a king to a particular city or locale.[19] Many New Testament writers use this term to designate the end-time appearance of the risen Christ in divine glory as the king and judge.[20] At Christ's parousia, he will raise the dead, carry

19. See "παρουσία," BAGD, 629–30.
20. See Matt. 24:3, 27, 37, 39; 1 Cor. 15:23; 1 Thess. 2:19; 3:13; 4:15; 5:23; 2 Thess. 2:1, 8; James 5:7–8; 2 Pet. 1:16; 3:4, 12; 1 John 2:28.

out the final judgment, fully realize and reveal the kingdom of God in the world, and bring his people to live eternally with him.

The future-looking tone of the name petition aligns with this future aspect of Christian eschatology. The name petition asks the Father to bring his plan of salvation to its full completion, and this is something that will happen at Christ's parousia. When the Father does this, he will manifest his holiness to all of creation.

This request for the Father to manifest his holiness fits with the references to "glory" in Jesus's teachings about the parousia.[21] Speaking of the parousia, Jesus states that the Son of Man will appear "in his glory" (Matt. 25:31), which is the same as the "glory of his Father" (16:27). In the Old Testament, the glory of the Lord was a sensible manifestation of the powerful, active presence of God.[22] The glory usually manifests in the phenomena of fire and cloud, and it does so, for instance, at Mount Sinai, in the wilderness tabernacle, and in Solomon's temple. The glory of the Lord is a revelation, a perceptible display of the presence and power of God. When the Lord Jesus appears at the parousia, he will appear "in his glory and the glory of the Father" (Luke 9:26). This end-time manifestation of Jesus in glory is at the same time a manifestation of the Father's glory and splendor; that is, when Jesus appears in glory at the parousia, the Father will show forth his holiness. Put differently, the Father will sanctify his name.

Ezekiel 36:23 speaks of God's action to sanctify his name in the end-time as his response to the profanation of his name caused by his people's sins. Through this gracious action of salvation, purification, and forgiveness, the Lord will show forth his holiness to all the nations of the world. Reading these texts within a post-resurrection context, we acknowledge that God has definitively dealt with the problem of sin in the death and resurrection of Jesus. And yet, through our sins and wickedness, we continue to dishonor God's name and create obstacles for people to come to know and honor him.

21. See Matt. 16:27; 18:38; 24:30; 25:31; Luke 9:26; 21:27.
22. Cf. Eichrodt, *Theology of the Old Testament*, 2:29–35.

Taking the name petition in tandem with Ezekiel 36:23, we can surmise that the display of the Father's holiness at the parousia will be so radiant that it will utterly burn away all the dishonor, confusion, and obscuring that our sins have caused. This action of the Father to sanctify his name and so reveal his holiness will leave no doubt that he is the Holy One, the one to whom the angels sing without end: "Holy, holy, holy, [is] the Lord God the Almighty, who was and is and is to come" (Rev. 4:8).

Throughout the divine economy, God reveals his goodness, power, and loving-kindness in the actions he works for his people. Many biblical texts present praise and worship as the proper response to these acts of God (e.g., Exod. 15:1–21; Rev. 5:9–14). The parousia will be the capstone of all the gracious and revelatory acts of God throughout the divine economy. Accordingly, when the Father brings his plan to its full completion at Christ's parousia and so manifests his holiness, the response of people will be to praise, worship, and honor the Father. This leads us to another element of the petition: *that people may rightly praise and honor him.*

We saw that the "sanctifying" of God's "name" is also something that God's people can do for him. In Isaiah 29:23, the Lord declares that after his eschatological action, his restored people "will sanctify my name; they will sanctify the Holy One of Jacob, and will stand in awe of the God of Israel." That is, the redeemed people of God can "sanctify" his name through their reverential obedience, proper praise, and gratitude (cf. Lev. 22:32).

The name petition suggests that the Father is the primary agent who will sanctify his name at the parousia. However, the plain sense of the Lord's Prayer can accommodate these insights from related biblical texts. And so, when the Father sanctifies his name by manifesting his holiness at the parousia, people will respond in turn by sanctifying his name through their reverence and praise.

Luke gives us an "anticipated participation" in this eschatological dynamic in the figure of Mary and her hymn of praise known as the Magnificat (Luke 1:46–55).[23] During her visit to her kinswoman Elizabeth, Mary sings this hymn. She praises God for the goodness he has shown her individually and the world as a whole in choosing her to be the mother of Jesus, whom she conceived in her womb by the power of the Holy Spirit. In this prayer, Mary states, "The Mighty One has done great things for me, and holy is his name" (1:49). The language of Mary's declaration "holy is his name" (*hagion to onoma autou*; 1:49) is very close to that of the Lord's Prayer: "Hallowed be your name" (*hagiasthētō to onoma sou*; 11:2). In fact, Mary's words here are the only instance in the Gospels where anybody declares that God's "name" is "holy" or "sanctified" (*hagios*). What the Lord's Prayer looks toward at the very end of days, Mary anticipates in her Magnificat: the Father manifests his holiness through his eschatological action in Christ, and people in turn praise and honor him and his name as holy.

Conclusion

Although it does not plainly pick up matters discussed elsewhere by Jesus, the name petition recalls select texts from the Old Testament Scriptures, such as Ezekiel 26:23 and Isaiah 29:23. These textual connections, along with the Greek syntax of the petition, give the name petition an eschatological tone. In this petition, we ask the Father to manifest his holiness by bringing his plan of salvation to its full completion at Christ's parousia. When the Father fully and plainly realizes in the world what has been accomplished in the death and resurrection of Jesus, his holiness will burn away all the confusion and obscuring of his goodness that our sins have caused. As a result, people will rightly praise and honor the Father. The Father will sanctify his name, and then people will sanctify the Father's name.

---

23. On the category "anticipated participation," see Wright and Martin, *Encountering the Living God*, 212; Martin, "Election, Covenant, and Law," 865–71, 886–90.

4

Kingdom and Will

As a request for the Father to bring his plan to its full completion, the name petition is a prayer for the parousia of Christ. The same can be said of the next petition in the Lord's Prayer: "Your kingdom come" (Matt. 6:10 // Luke 11:2). Both Matthew's version and Luke's version of the Lord's Prayer have the kingdom petition. Present only in Matthew is the will petition: "Your will be done, on earth as it is in heaven" (6:10). The will petition can be thought of as an interpretive expansion of the kingdom petition because the two are closely related in terms of content and theme. Accordingly, we will treat these two petitions together in a single chapter.

The kingdom of God (or as Matthew usually has it, the kingdom of heaven) is an overarching topic in Jesus's ministry, and so much of what Jesus says and does relates in some way to this reality. The Father's will is that which Jesus, the Father's obedient Son, teaches and does perfectly. Moreover, in Matthew, Jesus connects the Father's will and the kingdom by teaching that only those who do the Father's will (taught by Jesus) will enter the kingdom (7:21). Given the large amount of relevant material, we must be selective and focus on those matters that are most pertinent to our theological exposition of the kingdom and will petitions.

When we take these petitions in light of Jesus's ministry and their biblical allusions, *we can see them as requests for the Father to reveal and realize fully in the world his kingly rule in Christ and so transform the world such that the Father's will, which is now done perfectly in heaven, will be done perfectly in the world.*

Part 1: The Kingdom Petition

The Language of the Kingdom Petition

Matthew and Luke give the exact same reading of the kingdom petition: "Your kingdom come" (*elthetō hē basileia sou*; Matt. 6:10 // Luke 11:2). The Greek expression *hē basileia sou* means "your kingdom," and it is the subject of the verb *elthetō* ("come"). This verb is an aorist active imperative, which (as we have discussed) can be taken as asking for an action to be done on a single occasion. As with the name petition, the syntax of the verb gives this petition an eschatological tone. It looks for a time in the future when the Father's kingdom will come fully—that is, at Christ's parousia.

The kingdom petition invites us to register certain things about the Father and his kingdom and with respect to both the present and the future. For instance, the personal modifier "your" in the kingdom petition refers to the Father. He is the king who exercises sovereign rule, and his royal will is to be done. These affirmations should not be surprising given the well-established scriptural identification of the Lord, the God of Israel, as king.[1] Moreover, the kingdom petition implies that the Father's kingdom is a reality that is in some respects *not* present. If the Father's kingdom was something fully present in the world, Jesus would not be instructing us to pray for it to "come" (since it would already be here completely). Moreover, the verb "come" suggests that the Father's kingdom is something that (to put it in spatial terms) enters the world from without. It is a reality that does not originate in the world but enters into the world

---

1. Kohler, "Ahabah Rabbah."

(cf. John 18:36–37). In the kingdom petition, Jesus teaches us to ask the Father to make his kingly rule fully present and realized in the world.

Exposition of the Kingdom Petition

Witness from the Scriptures

The kingdom petition recalls the scriptural teaching that God is king and that he has promised to act as king in the end-time to put things right. Throughout the Old Testament Scriptures, we find the teaching that the Lord (YHWH), the God of Israel, is king. From the creation narratives to covenant legislation to the Wisdom literature, this claim is articulated in a variety of ways. The kingship of God is a prominent topic in the book of Psalms, and the psalms allow us to sketch out key aspects of the biblical picture of God as the king.

"YHWH Reigns!"—Testimony from the Psalms

The psalms teach that the Lord is the king and has always been the king (9:7; 10:16; 29:10; 93:2).[2] Many psalms associate the Lord's kingship with his role as the Creator (24:1–10; 89:8–14; 95:3–6; 96:5). As the Creator of all things, the Lord is also the sovereign ruler of all things, including all peoples: the Lord is king both of Israel (89:18; 95:6–7; 99) and of all the nations (47:1–2, 8–9). As part of being king, the Lord is also a warrior (89:9–12; 93:1; 97:10). Since the Lord is the king of all, the psalms teach that the proper responses to the Lord are to recognize his sovereign authority, to pay him homage, and to obey his kingly will (47:1–2, 8–9; 89:15–16; 95:1–7; 96:7–9; 99:3, 5).

The Lord is the king of Israel in a special way by virtue of his covenant with them. Recalling ancient Near Eastern treaty formulas, many covenant texts present the Lord as a king who enters into a sacred relationship with a lesser party (i.e., Israel) who owes him allegiance and obedience.[3] Old Testament texts also present the Lord as

---

2. McCann, *Book of Psalms*, 667–68, 1053; Levenson, *Love of God*, 2.

3. For a helpful introduction to this well-attested point, see Hillers, *Covenant*, esp. 25–45.

exercising his kingly rule through the Davidic monarch. The Lord has chosen the Davidic dynasty to rule over Israel (2 Sam. 7:8–17; Ps. 89). Through the Davidic royal line, God will exercise his kingly power to lead his people and save them from their enemies (Pss. 2:8–9; 89:22–24). While the Old Testament Scriptures do not often speak of God's "kingdom," the term does occur in 1–2 Chronicles, where it is identified with the kingdom of Israel ruled by the Davidic king (1 Chron. 28:5; 2 Chron. 13:8).

There are two related "spaces" from which the Lord exercises his kingly rule. For one, the psalms speak of God as reigning from his throne in heaven, the customary spatial image for God's dwelling (Pss. 11:4; 33:13–14).[4] The Lord has also chosen to dwell among his people Israel in earthly sanctuaries—the wilderness tabernacle and then the Jerusalem temple. These are regarded as sensible, worldly replicas of God's heavenly temple-palace (cf. Exod. 25:8–9; Wis. 9:8, 10). As the place where the king dwells in a unique way on earth, the Jerusalem temple is the other place from which the Lord reigns as king (Ps. 24). Several of the psalms employ a phrase, "YHWH reigns!" (my translation; Hb. *YHWH mālāk*), which is thought to be an acclamation of the Lord's kingship made in the temple liturgy.[5]

As king of all, the Lord governs the world by his will and enforces it as judge. The angels do the Lord's will in heaven (Ps. 103:20–21), and on earth, the Lord has taught his will to Israel in a special way by giving them the Torah (e.g., 147:19–20; cf. 80:8; 119:142). The psalms emphasize strongly that God's kingly will is moral (89:14; 96:10; 98:9; 99:4). Psalm 99 states, "Mighty King, lover of justice, you have established equity; you have executed justice and righteousness in

4. Some cosmological accounts in Scripture and the biblical tradition speak of the heavens as a separate realm over which the Lord sits enthroned (e.g., Ps. 113:5–6).

5. See Pss. 93:1; 96:10; 97:1; 99:1; cf. 1 Chron. 16:31; Isa. 24:23. This phrase can also be translated in the sense of "YHWH has become king." This interpretation views the phrase in light of ancient Near Eastern creation theology wherein the hero god is acclaimed king upon defeating the forces of chaos and thus bringing stability to the world. On this phrase (and the rationale for so translating it), see McCann, *Book of Psalms*, 1053. Cf. Blenkinsopp, *Isaiah 40–55*, 342–43.

Jacob" (v. 4). It is according to the moral standard of his will that God carries out judgment: "He will judge the world with righteousness, and the peoples with his truth" (96:13; cf. 98:9).

At the same time, there is a vivid awareness that the Lord's kingly rule is contested and opposed in the world. Drawing on ancient Near Eastern religious imagery, the psalms present "the seas" (i.e., the primordial forces of chaos) as battling against the Lord (Pss. 89:9–10; 93:3–4) and the gods of the nations as his rivals (29:1–2; 96:4–5; 97:7–9).[6] Moreover, the psalms recognize that there are all kinds of ways the Lord's kingly will is *not* done in the world: sin and injustice abound, and those who so act seem to do it with impunity (94:1–7); idolators worship other gods (97:7); wicked people deny that the Lord cares—or even exists (10:4; 14:1–3; 94:3–7); the Lord's own people sin against him (95:8–11; 99:8), and they experience sufferings, defeats, and exile (44:11; 89:39–45). Sin, evil, and injustice are all forms of rebellion against the heavenly king, for they all run contrary to his sovereign, righteous will.

Psalms that both recall the Lord's past actions as king and lament the various sufferings, injustices, and forms of wickedness in the world can serve as an invitation for God to once again act as king (e.g., Pss. 44:23–26; 89:46–51). By recounting those times when God acted as king in the past, the psalms voice a confident hope that God will once again act as king to put things right.[7] Such hope for God to again act as king also finds expression in biblical texts that speak of God's eschatological action and that do so with specific reference to God's kingship or kingdom. While several important examples can be cited, we will focus on a key witness that speaks of God's action to bring his kingdom to the world: the book of Daniel.[8]

6. Clifford, *Creation Accounts*, 117–33, 151–62.
7. Clifford, *Psalms 73–150*, 95.
8. Although space does not permit discussion of all these texts, important in this regard are (1) the proclamation of the Lord's kingship in connection with his action to return to his exiled people and bring about the restoration of Israel (Isa. 52:7–10) and (2) the appearance of the Lord as a warrior-king in Zech. 14 to deliver a suffering Jerusalem from its enemies.

The Book of Daniel: "The God of Heaven Will Set Up a Kingdom"

The book of Daniel is an apocalyptic writing that is set during the Babylonian exile but speaks to the time of the Maccabean revolt (ca. 168–164 BC).[9] Daniel is the book in the Old Testament that speaks most prominently about God's kingdom (2:44; 4:3, 34; 6:26; 7:14, 27), and it emphasizes his cosmic and all-encompassing sovereignty.

There are several things to highlight about the presentation of God's kingdom in Daniel. First, God's kingdom is primarily centered in heaven. Like the psalms, Daniel identifies heaven as the place where God sets his throne (Dan. 3:54–56 LXX; Pr. Azar. 32–34). On multiple occasions in Daniel, God is called "the God of heaven" (2:18–19, 37, 44; cf. 5:23), a title that underscores God's reign as king from heaven.[10]

Second, the kingly rule of God is both eternal and all-encompassing. God is king from all eternity, and there is nothing that is not subject to his sovereign rule (Dan. 4:17, 25). Statements about the eternity and universality of God's kingship are often made in Daniel by gentile kings. After they witness a display of God's power, given through Daniel and his companions, these gentile kings acknowledge supremacy of Israel's God over all—including themselves as kings on earth. For instance, after seeing Daniel's miraculous deliverance from death in the lions' den, King Darius confesses the sovereignty of Israel's God: "He is the living God, enduring forever. His kingdom shall never be destroyed, and his dominion has no end" (6:26; cf. 4:3, 34).

Third, in the end-time, God is going to act decisively to do away with all worldly kingdoms and rule perfectly on earth as king. As acknowledged in the psalms, the Lord is king over all, but his kingly rule is opposed in the world. Daniel enhances these claims to show that God will act as king in the end-time to defeat all rivals to his

---

9. At the time when Daniel was completed, Jews in the land of Israel were undergoing a severe persecution by the Greco-Syrian king Antiochus IV, who had outlawed Jewish religious practices under penalty of death. Many Jews chose to remain faithful to their practices, traditions, and beliefs rather than acquiesce to the king's policies. Thus, they were executed and died as martyrs.

10. Pennington, *Heaven and Earth*, 290–91.

kingly rule and set up his eternal and universal sovereignty in the world. Different expressions of this eschatological scenario appear in Daniel.[11]

One version of this scenario is the dream vision of the statue given in Daniel 2. King Nebuchadnezzar of Babylon has an upsetting dream that Daniel proceeds to recount and interpret through a revelation from God. Daniel reports that in his dream, the king saw a giant statue, whose body was composed of several different materials of descending value from top to bottom (i.e., golden head, silver chest and arms, bronze midsection, iron legs, and feet of a blend of iron and clay). Next, the king saw that "a stone was cut out, not by human hands" (2:34), which hit the statue's feet, smashing them into bits. The entire statue then collapsed into dust, which was blown away in the wind. Finally, "the stone that struck the statue became a great mountain and filled the whole earth" (2:35).

Daniel teaches that the composite statue represents a series of worldly kingdoms, with Nebuchadnezzar of Babylon being the golden head (Dan. 2:38).[12] Especially significant in this sequence is the stone that destroys the statue and then expands to become a mountain filling the world. The stone is implied to represent God's action. Since the stone was hewn, but not by a human hand, the text implies that the stone was cut by God's hand.[13] So understood, God will act decisively in the end-time to do away with the kingdoms of the world and put down all rivals to his kingship.[14] Expanding into a mountain, the stone is the kingdom set up by God, for it fills the whole world and lasts forever: "And in the days of those kings the God of heaven will set up a kingdom that shall never be destroyed, nor shall this kingdom be left to another people. It shall crush all

11. N. T. Wright, *New Testament*, 291–97, 313–14.
12. A series of other kingdoms follows his rule, with the last one in the sequence being the blend of iron and clay—arguably the Hellenistic kingdoms after Alexander the Great, over which Antiochus IV was a king.
13. This exemplifies the Semitic use of the passive voice, discussed in chap. 3, known as the divine passive.
14. Pennington, *Heaven and Earth*, 268–78.

these kingdoms and bring them to an end, and it shall stand forever" (2:44).

Daniel 7 gives us a similar account, although with different emphases and images. In the first part, Daniel sees a series of four monsters that are said to be four kings and kingdoms (7:17, 23). The fourth monster/kingdom is especially evil, for it blasphemes God and violently persecutes his people (7:25). The series of monsters and the havoc they cause come to an end when God acts in the end-time as the king and judge (7:9–12). Without any drama or struggle, God pronounces judgment on the monsters, deposing and destroying them. As in the statue vision (Dan. 2), God deposes all rival powers in the world, and he reigns forever over earth. Moreover, God vindicates his faithful people and shares his universal, kingly rule with them, who are personified in the figure of "the Son of Man" (7:13–14). The text states, "The kingship and dominion and the greatness of the kingdoms under the whole heaven shall be given to the people of the holy ones of the Most High; their kingdom shall be an everlasting kingdom, and all dominions shall serve and obey them" (7:27).

Daniel 12 provides another account, albeit in a more compressed form. Significant for our purposes is the introduction into this eschatological scenario of the resurrection of the dead. That is, when God acts to put an end to the present evil age, he will resurrect the dead and carry out the end-time judgment: "Many of those who sleep in the dust of the earth shall awake, some to everlasting life, and some to shame and everlasting contempt" (Dan. 12:2). The wicked will be damned, but the righteous will be given a heavenly, glorified mode of life with God: they "shall shine like the brightness of the sky . . . like the stars forever and ever" (12:3). Resurrection to glorified life is the mode of life proper to the future age to come, otherwise known as the kingdom of God.

This brief examination of key biblical texts reminds us that if we are to understand Jesus's teaching about the kingdom of God, we need to recognize that this topic is deeply embedded in the Scriptures and spirituality of Israel. Throughout the Scriptures, the Lord is recognized as the king (despite the many problems in the world), and scenarios of God's eschatological action announce that he will act definitively as king in the end-time to put things right. Such scenarios announce that in the end-time, God will act to save his people and defeat their enemies, to make all things right and just, and to transform the world permanently under his immediate and unopposed sovereignty. The kingdom of God is an *eschatological* reality that God brings about through his kingly action and rule. This is what Jesus teaches is happening in him and his ministry when he announces, "The kingdom of God has come near" (Mark 1:15).

The Good News of the Kingdom of God

The kingdom petition fits within the larger body of Jesus's teaching on the kingdom of God. His declaration "The kingdom of heaven has come near" recalls these biblical promises and announces their fulfillment (Matt. 4:17; 10:7; cf. Mark 1:15; Luke 10:9; 10:11). That is, God in Jesus is definitively acting in power as king to make good on what he promised to do in the end-time: to forgive his people and deliver them from the hands of their enemies, to bring justice to the world and put things right, and to transform the world under his sovereignty.

Throughout the Gospels, Jesus teaches about the kingdom of God in both words (e.g., parables and short sayings) and actions (e.g., miracles and prophetic gestures). His teaching about the kingdom is complex, enigmatic, and even somewhat paradoxical.[15] He speaks of the kingdom of God as a reality that is in some respects something present (Matt. 12:28; Luke 17:21) and in other respects something future (Matt. 6:10; 16:28). The kingdom is in some ways associated with the Davidic monarchy and God's promises to restore it under a messiah-king (Matt. 16:19; Luke 1:32–33), and the kingdom is also a

---

15. The kingdom of God has been the subject of much discussion and debate, with different assessments and interpretations of the evidence being proposed. For discussions of the issues and evidence, see Perrin, *Kingdom of God*; Meier, *Marginal Jew*, 2:237–506; Allison, *Constructing Jesus*, 164–204; Black, *Lord's Prayer*, 108–34.

transcendent, heavenly realm (Matt. 5:34; 23:22; 25:34). The kingdom is a reality into which people enter or from which they are excluded (Matt. 25:34, 41, 46). The kingdom has a hierarchy (Matt. 5:19; 19:28; Luke 22:30) in which the humble and self-sacrificing have high rank (Matt. 18:1–4; 20:26–28). The coming of God's kingdom is good news for the poor (Luke 6:20), the piously dependent (Matt. 5:3), and those who are persecuted for the sake of what is good (Matt. 5:10). The kingdom is closely correlated with people's conduct (Matt. 7:21), and it is also a gift from the Father (Luke 12:32) that people must receive (Matt. 19:11–12 // Luke 18:17). Jesus teaches "the mysteries of the kingdom" (Matt. 13:11)[16] by using familiar yet often elusive images such as a mustard seed (Matt. 13:31–32 // Luke 13:19), yeast in dough (Matt. 13:33 // Luke 13:21), and a great dinner banquet (Matt. 8:11; 22:1–14). The kingdom is present in the community of Jesus's disciples—the church—and yet the kingdom cannot be wholly identified with the church in every respect (Matt. 13:40–43; 16:18–19; Luke 17:20–21).

Important for our purposes are the enigmatic ways Jesus talks about the kingdom, especially concerning its time and place.[17] Jesus teaches that the kingdom of God is a reality that is in some respects present, here and now, in him and his ministry. But there are other aspects of the kingdom that are heavenly or transcendent (space) and are yet to come in the future (time).

To begin with, Jesus teaches that the kingdom of God—the end-time action of God as king and its resulting state of affairs—is in some respects actively present in him and his ministry.[18] The presence and power of the kingdom of God are instantiated in Jesus's miracles. On several occasions, Matthew associates Jesus's teaching "the good news of the kingdom" with his actions to heal sick people (4:23; 9:35). In Luke 10, when Jesus dispatches the seventy-two dis-

16. Here and elsewhere the translation "the mysteries of the kingdom of heaven" is my translation of *ta mystēria tēs basileias tōn ouranōn* in Matt. 13:11.
17. Following here the basic template of Sanders, *Historical Figure of Jesus*, 170–76.
18. Cf. Meier, *Marginal Jew*, 2:398–506.

ciples, he instructs them that upon entering a welcoming place, they are to "cure the sick who are there, and say to them, 'The kingdom of God has come near to you'" (v. 9). Matthew and Luke both show the association of the kingdom of God with Jesus's exorcisms. Both evangelists record a saying of Jesus in which he interprets the significance of his exorcism ministry: "If it is by the Spirit of God that I cast out demons, then the kingdom of God has come upon you" (Matt. 12:28; cf. Luke 11:20). Some eschatological scenarios in Scripture present God as a warrior-king who will defeat his enemies and deliver his people from their power (e.g., Isa. 52:7–12; Dan. 7:11–12; Zech. 14:1–21). Taken in this light, Jesus acts here as the divine warrior-king who defeats his enemies (i.e., the demons) and rescues his people from their power. In these miracles, God is acting in power as king to heal his people, save them from the power of their enemies, and end Satan's dominion in the world.

Luke emphasizes the arrival of the eschatological, messianic age with Jesus in the programmatic scene that opens his account of Jesus's ministry: Jesus's rejection in the Nazareth synagogue (Luke 4:14–30). During the synagogue liturgy, Jesus reads a selection from Isaiah that speaks of the saving acts to be performed by the one bearing the Lord's Spirit: "To bring good news to the poor . . . to proclaim release to the captives and recovery of sight to the blind, to let the oppressed go free, to proclaim a year of the Lord's favor" (4:18–19). After reading this text, Jesus tells his hearers, "Today this scripture has been fulfilled in your hearing" (4:21). Jesus announces that God's promises in Scripture are now being realized in him. The arrival of the messianic age in Jesus means that God is coming to help the helpless, to heal the afflicted, and to put things right in the world. This is "the good news of the kingdom of God" (4:43).

While teaching that the kingdom is in some respects actively present in him and his ministry, Jesus also teaches that the kingdom of God has future aspects.[19] This is intimated in some of the so-called growth parables. In the parable of the mustard seed, for instance,

19. See Meier, *Marginal Jew*, 2:289–397.

Jesus speaks of the kingdom of God as a present reality that grows toward a future state (Matt. 13:31–32 // Luke 13:18–19). The kingdom is like a mustard seed in that it begins very small, but it grows to become "the greatest of shrubs and becomes a tree" in which birds can nest (Matt. 13:32). Like the divinely cut stone that smashes the statue and develops into the world-filling mountain that is God's everlasting kingdom (Dan. 2:44), the mustard seed that is the kingdom present in Jesus's ministry begins small but will grow into a future fullness.[20]

The connection between the present and the future aspects of the kingdom also appears in the Beatitudes (Matt. 5:3–12 // Luke 6:20–23). Many of the Beatitudes feature a contrast between the present and the future—for example, "Blessed *are* those who mourn, for they *will be* comforted" (Matt. 5:4, emphasis added; cf. Luke 6:21). Jesus declares certain virtues or states to be "blessed" *now* because they will be either reversed or rewarded in the *future* when the kingdom of God becomes fully realized in the world. In particular, Jesus singles out "the poor" (or "the poor in spirit") as those who possess the kingdom of God (Matt. 5:3 // Luke 6:20).[21] Those who are poor and dependent on God are now blessed because this present state is correlated with the future dimensions of the kingdom. The kingdom thus entails God's action to put things right in the world, to comfort those afflicted (e.g., with poverty, mourning, hunger), and to bless and reward conduct that is right, just, and pleasing to him (e.g., humility, hungering for righteousness, showing mercy, devotion to God, peacemaking, being persecuted for the sake of righteousness and of Jesus).

Jesus also promises future blessings and rewards in the kingdom of God for those who follow him now with faith and discipleship. Responding to Peter's question as to what he and the other apostles will receive from Jesus since they have given up everything for him

---

20. Jeremias, *Parables of Jesus*, 149; Meier, *Marginal Jew*, 5:239.
21. In Matthew, Jesus also pronounces those "who are persecuted for righteousness' sake" as "blessed" and as possessing "the kingdom of heaven" (5:10). The use of poverty as a spiritual category to denote devotion and piety is indebted to Zeph. 3:12–13.

(Matt. 19:27; cf. Luke 18:28), Jesus promises that they will share in his kingly rule and have positions of authority in the kingdom: "At the renewal of all things, when the Son of Man is seated on the throne of his glory, you who have followed me will also sit on twelve thrones, judging the twelve tribes of Israel" (Matt. 19:28; cf. Luke 22:28–30). The future state of affairs that is the kingdom of God will be the new creation, a "renewal of all things" (Matt. 19:28); it is the apocalyptic "age to come" (Luke 18:30). In this future state of affairs, Jesus will sit on his throne, and the apostles will share in his sovereign rule by sitting on thrones themselves. Jesus goes on to say that those who give up goods of the world (e.g., family and property) for his sake will receive "eternal life" in the kingdom of God (Matt. 19:29 // Luke 18:29–30). Here the kingdom comes to light as a future reality with its own goods, and these goods are superior to even the greatest goods (i.e., family and friends) in the present state of affairs. The kingdom of God means a renewal on a cosmic scale, eternal life with God, and a share in Jesus's kingly rule.

The kingdom of God is the eschatological action of God as king and the resulting state of affairs under his sovereignty. This definitive, end-time saving action of God the king is the death and resurrection of Jesus. The Gospel passion narratives in various ways emphasize that Jesus is the king in the events of his suffering and death. Jesus's act of perfect love and obedience on the cross deals with the problem of sin, effecting the "ransom" of sinners from sin and its punishment (Matt. 20:28). It is this act of Jesus, moreover, that breaks the dominion of the devil over sinners (John 12:31). In the resurrection, Jesus is raised to an eschatological mode of life, and his humanity is totally transformed by divine glory. He has entered into the mode of embodied, eternal life with God that was promised to the righteous in Daniel 12 and that marks the future age to come—that is, the kingdom of God. The resurrection of Jesus is the kingdom of God taking irrevocable root in the world, and the glorification of his humanity is the anchor point for the transformation of creation to come.

When we speak of the "kingdom" in the Lord's Prayer, we recall Jesus's kingdom of God ministry. This entails that God in Jesus is fulfilling his promises to act as king in the end-time and that these realities have in some ways become present in the world. In particular, through the life, death, and resurrection of Jesus, God has worked his definitive, end-time saving act as king and has permanently planted in the world the eschatological reality of his sovereignty. The kingdom of God has, in some respects, become a present reality, although it still has elements that are temporally future. It is with these future aspects of the kingdom of God that the kingdom petition is primarily concerned.

Your Kingdom Come

When we pray "Your kingdom come," we ask the Father to reveal and realize fully in the world his kingly rule in Christ and so transform the world. At the end of Matthew's Gospel, the risen Jesus tells the apostles, "I am with you always, to the end of the age" (28:20). The risen Jesus promises to remain always with his disciples in the church (Matt. 18:20; 28:20), and through his abiding presence and holiness in the church, the kingdom of God is, genuinely though mysteriously, present and active in the world. Having poured out the Holy Spirit on his disciples, the risen Jesus makes available to people the realities of heavenly, eschatological life—that is, life in the kingdom of God—which we come to enjoy through our communion with him in the church (Acts 2:33, 38; 1 Cor. 1:9; 12:12–13; 1 John 1:3). At the same time, the risen Jesus also points his apostles to a moment in the future: the end of the age. This comment picks up the future dimensions to God's saving action in Christ; there is something yet to come.

There are three other places in Matthew where the expression "the end of the age" appears (13:40, 49; 24:3). These passages all concern the same future moment when what has been done in Christ will be fully realized and the kingdom will be revealed in all its fullness: Christ's parousia.

As the end-time appearance of the risen Jesus in glory, the parousia is when the divine plan of salvation reaches its full completion (e.g., Matt. 13:39–43; 16:27; 25:31–46; Luke 9:26; 21:27). There are numerous associations between Jesus's parousia and kingship. The Synoptics all speak of the Son of Man appearing in "glory" at his parousia (Matt. 16:27; Mark 13:26; Luke 21:27), and Matthew in particular speaks of Jesus as sitting on a "throne" (25:31; cf. 19:28). At the parousia, the glorified Jesus will exercise the kingly prerogative of carrying out the final judgment (Matt. 13:41–43; 25:31–46).[22] As the judge, the glorified Jesus will admit or exclude people from his Father's kingdom based on what we do or fail to do to him as present in the needy (Matt. 25:34, 40, 45–46). Those admitted into the kingdom will enjoy eternal, eschatological life with God: "The righteous will shine like the sun in the kingdom of their Father" (Matt. 13:43; cf. Dan. 12:3).

Luke's Gospel similarly associates the parousia with the culmination of the divine plan and the full establishment of the kingdom of God. In Luke's version of Jesus's eschatological discourse in Jerusalem, Jesus says, "They will see 'the Son of Man coming in a cloud' with power and great glory. Now when you see these things begin to take place, . . . your redemption is drawing near" (21:27–28). In the parable of the fig tree, which follows this teaching about the parousia, Jesus teaches, "When you see these things taking place, you know that the kingdom of God is near" (21:31). With Christ's parousia, God's saving plans are brought to their full completion, and the kingdom of God becomes present and manifest in all its fullness and splendor (Luke 18:29–30; cf. Matt. 12:32).

Christians believe that at Christ's parousia those things that the Scriptures connect with the eschatological action of God as king and that Jesus himself associates with the future aspects of the kingdom— for example, the elimination of sin, evil, and injustice; the general resurrection and judgment; the transformation of the world; the

---

22. Cf. 1 En. 69:26–29, where the heavenly figure of the Son of Man carries out the end-time judgment while seated on a glorious throne.

granting of eternal, eschatological life with God and heavenly blessings to the righteous and faithful—will take place. What has been accomplished in the life, death, and resurrection of Jesus will be fully realized and revealed in the world. This is what we ask for when we pray, "Your kingdom come."

Part 2: The Will Petition

The Language of the Will Petition

Only Matthew's version of the Lord's Prayer contains the will petition: "Your will be done, on earth as it is in heaven" (*genēthētō to thelēma sou, hōs en ouranō kai epi gēs*; 6:10). The will petition has two component phrases. The first part has a similar construction to the other "you" petitions: it begins with the aorist imperative "be done" (*genēthētō*) and then gives the subject "your will" (*to thelēma sou*). The aorist imperative looks for an action to be completed on a single occasion, and this verb gives the will petition a similarly eschatological perspective as the other "you" petitions.

The second part of the will petition is an adverb phrase concerning the doing of the Father's will. Here we need to register a difference between the Greek text and its usual English translation. The customary English rendering of the phrase is "on earth as it is in heaven." This translation, however, does not reflect the ordering of the words in the Greek text. The Greek adverb phrase in Matthew's Gospel—*hōs en ouranō kai epi gēs*—sequentially reads "as in heaven so also upon earth." The sequence of the words is significant. By leading with the expression "as in heaven" (*hōs en ouranō*), the petition establishes "heaven" (*ouranō*) both as the realm where the Father's will is done and as the measure for doing the Father's will.[23] That is, the petition asks that just "as" the Father's will is now done in heaven, so may his will be done "also on earth" (my translation; Gk. *kai epi gēs*).

23. So too Davies and Allison, *Gospel according to Saint Matthew*, 1:606; Luz, *Matthew 1–7*, 319.

The will petition articulates a series of contrasts. First, there is a contrast of spaces—namely, "heaven" and "earth." Second, there is a contrast of situations in those two spaces. The heavenly situation is one in which the Father's will is done perfectly. The situation on earth, however, is different. Similar to the kingdom petition, the will petition implies that there are ways the Father's will is *not* done on earth as it is in heaven. If the Father's will was already done on earth as it is in heaven (i.e., perfectly), there would be no need for us to pray for this to occur. But just as there are ways the kingdom is not yet fully realized in the world, so too are there ways the Father's will is not yet done on earth as it is in heaven. Third, the petition implies a contrast concerning time.[24] In the present time, the Father's will is done perfectly in heaven, but it is not done perfectly on earth. The will petition asks the Father to change this present situation on earth. It envisions a future time when the Father will see to it that the current situation in heaven (i.e., his will being done perfectly) will also come to be on earth.

Exposition of the Will Petition

When we pray "Your will be done, on earth as it is in heaven," we ask that the Father's will, which is now done perfectly in heaven, will be done perfectly in the world. This claim can be further specified, and here we identify two aspects of the will petition.

First, in the will petition, we pray for a specific component in the full realization of the kingdom of God: the securing of perfect goodness in the world and the complete removal of evil. The will petition presupposes much of what we saw in the psalms about God's kingly rule. The psalms present the Lord reigning as king over all from his heavenly throne. Heaven is the realm where the Lord's kingship is honored and unopposed and where his angelic ministers carry out

---

24. In a strict theological sense, "time" (and temporal terms like "before" and "after") does not apply to God's eternity, since time is a dimension and property of creation. As Augustine (*City of God* 11.6) states, "The world was not made in time but with time" (Babcock, 220).

his sovereign will perfectly. Psalm 103:19–21 articulates this heavenly situation:

> The LORD has established his throne in the heavens,
>   and his kingdom rules over all.
> Bless the LORD, O you his angels,
>   you mighty ones who do his bidding,
>   obedient to his spoken word.
> Bless the LORD, all his hosts,
>   his ministers that do his will.

This psalm presents God as the heavenly king who rules supreme over all creation, and it calls on the angels to praise him. The psalmist addresses the angels with several parallel terms and titles—"angels," "mighty ones," "his hosts," "ministers"—that identify them as servants of the heavenly king. The psalmist also names several parallel actions of the Lord's angelic ministers that are all performed in relation to the Lord's will: they "do his bidding"; they are "obedient to his spoken word"; they "do his will." This psalm thus presents the Lord as the king who reigns supreme from his heavenly throne and whose angelic servants carry out his will perfectly and without fail. Heaven is where the Lord's kingship is honored, and his will is done perfectly.

As we also saw in the psalms, the Lord's kingly will is perfectly good, moral, and just. In Psalm 97, the psalmist declares, "Righteousness and justice are the foundation of his throne" and later adds, "The heavens proclaim his righteousness" (vv. 2, 6; cf. 89:14). A cluster of royal psalms that celebrate the Lord's kingship (Pss. 93, 95–99) declare that the ways of the Lord are uprightness or "equity" (96:10; 98:9; 99:4), "righteousness" (96:13; 97:2, 6; 98:9; 99:4), and "justice" (97:2; 99:4). The Lord is a "lover of justice" (99:4), and he "loves those who hate evil" (97:10). He has "steadfast love and faithfulness" to Israel (98:3). As Israel's covenantal sovereign, the Lord teaches his will to Israel in a unique way by giving them the Torah (147:19–20). As the Lord's covenantal subject, Israel honors his sovereignty by their fidelity and obedience to his will, which is given in the Torah.

While God's good and righteous will is done perfectly in heaven, the same cannot be said of earth. In the world, human beings, who have been created by God and are naturally subject to him as their Creator and Lord, disobey his will by committing sin. Our sins are acts of rebellion and opposition to God's kingly rule. Through our sin, we assert ourselves over and against God and try to refuse what we naturally and inescapably are: his creatures and subjects. Sin is an act of rebellion in which we refuse the sovereignty of God and assert the sovereignty of the self. The presence in the world of evil, sin, and injustice and the widespread havoc that our sinful acts generate are all instances and indicators of the Father's will *not* being done on earth as in heaven.

Evil, sin, and injustice are thus markers of the state of affairs existing in contradistinction to the kingdom of God (or kingdom of heaven). In an apocalyptic register, these are features of the present evil age: the cosmic state of affairs wherein the wicked prosper and the righteous suffer, where injustice and evil abound, and in which the devil—the foremost rebel among God's creatures—has been granted a certain measure of dominion over the world. Our sinful refusal to do the Father's will is part of the problem that the establishment of the kingdom of God solves.

Matthew's Gospel presents elements that square with this account of God's kingship and will. Recalling the scriptural presentation of heaven as the seat of God's kingship, Jesus refers to "heaven" as God's throne (Matt. 5:34; cf. 23:22). Matthew uses the phrase "the kingdom of heaven" (4:17) much more than "the kingdom of God."[25] Matthew uses this descriptor, as Jonathan Pennington argues, to emphasize the heavenly transcendence of God's kingdom and to contrast it with kingdoms of the earth.[26] Matthew's version of the opening address of the Lord's Prayer likewise locates the Father "in heaven" (6:9).

25. Matthew uses the expression "the kingdom of God" in 12:28; 19:24; 21:31, 43.
26. Pennington, *Heaven and Earth*, 342.

The will petition fills out this picture by identifying heaven both as the space where the Father's will is now done and as the basis for praying that the Father's "will be done, on earth as it is in heaven" (6:10). Matthew thus presents the Father reigning as king over all from his heavenly throne, and he presents heaven as the space where the Father's will is rightly done. This is the sovereignty of God that enters eschatologically into the world with Jesus as he announces, "The kingdom of heaven has come near" (4:17).

As discussed in chapter 1, a key dimension of the Sermon on the Mount, wherein Matthew locates the Lord's Prayer, is Jesus's teaching about "righteousness"—that is, the uprightness of living that is pleasing to God. In Jewish tradition, such conduct is prescribed in the Torah. In the Sermon on the Mount, Jesus gives his teaching on righteousness, which is the fulfillment of Torah (Matt. 5:18). Jesus teaches at length about the conduct his disciples must live out, and he explicitly connects such righteous conduct with the kingdom of heaven. Near the beginning of the sermon, Jesus remarks, "For I tell you, unless your righteousness exceeds that of the scribes and Pharisees, you will never enter the kingdom of heaven" (5:20). And near the sermon's end, Jesus similarly teaches, "Not everyone who says to me, 'Lord, Lord,' will enter the kingdom of heaven, but only the one who does the will of my Father in heaven" (7:21).

Jesus's teaching on righteous conduct can be understood as his teaching about conduct that conforms to the Father's kingly will. The psalms repeatedly identify God's kingly will and ways as "righteousness" (Pss. 96:13; 97:2, 6; 98:9; 99:4), and thus conduct that conforms to God's kingly will is similarly righteous. Accordingly, those virtues and practices that Jesus teaches in the Sermon on the Mount constitute a righteous life lived in obedience to the Father's will. That is, it is life that honors the Father's kingly rule—the life of the kingdom of heaven.

We can see how the will petition is an interpretive expansion of the kingdom petition. It is a prayer that "the kingdom of heaven"—where the Father's kingly rule is perfectly recognized and honored and his will is completely obeyed—will be realized in the world. It is a prayer that the Father's goodness, justice, and righteousness will completely and forever pervade the world.

While we live after God's definitive end-time saving act—the death and resurrection of Jesus—we can readily see how the Father's will is *not* done on earth: sin and evil remain, injustice and suffering abound, and the sovereignty of God is still opposed. The will petition asks the Father to change this by fully realizing and revealing his kingly rule in the world. The will petition, like the kingdom petition, is a prayer for Jesus's parousia and the state of affairs it will bring about.

Since it involves the full realization of the kingdom of God in the world, the parousia will also feature the securing of perfect goodness in the world and the complete removal of evil. Matthew's Gospel recognizes that in the present time both the world and the church are mixed groups, for they are composed of both good and evil people, wheat and weeds (13:36–43). At the parousia, the risen Jesus will secure goodness and righteousness in the eschatological state of affairs by carrying out the last judgment. Here, the enthroned Jesus will separate the wheat and the weeds, "the children of the kingdom" and "the children of the evil one" (13:38), the sheep and the goats (25:31–46). Passing judgment on all according to their conduct—that is, their obedience or lack thereof to the Father's kingly will (cf. 16:27; 25:34–46)—he will order his angels to remove "all causes of sin and all evildoers" and to "throw them into the furnace of fire" (13:41–42). To those who honor the Father's kingship by obeying his will, the glorified Jesus will grant heavenly life "in the kingdom of their Father" (13:43; cf. 25:34–40). When those who oppose the Father's kingship by refusing to do his will are sent "into the eternal fire prepared for the devil and his angels" (25:41) after Christ's parousia, all that will remain is goodness and righteousness—life in the eternal kingdom of God, fully realized and revealed in the world.

When the Father fully establishes and manifests his kingly rule in the world, then his will will "be done, on earth as it is in heaven" (Matt. 6:10). That is, the Father's kingly will is going to be done in the world perfectly, completely, and unopposed. The willing obedience that characterizes heaven now will come to exist in the world in the future. At that time, sin, wickedness, evil, injustice, and immorality will be no more, and God's will, which is righteousness, justice, truth, love, and goodness, will reign perfectly. The will petition is a request for the Father to transform the earth so that it will be like heaven.

Second, in the will petition, we pray to become obedient as Jesus is obedient. Arguably, the most vivid narrative display of what the will petition envisions is Jesus praying in Gethsemane (Matt. 26:36–46). As the Lord's Prayer begins with the address "our Father," so Jesus begins his prayer in Gethsemane with the address "my Father" (26:39, 42). He asks the Father "if it is possible" that "this cup pass" (26:39). In the Scriptures, the "cup" is often an image of what God has in store for someone (Pss. 11:6; 16:5), and in this sense, it can be understood as what God wills. While Jesus naturally recoils from the prospect of his imminent suffering and death, he consents to the Father's will and prays, "Not what I want but what you want" (Matt. 26:39). Following Mark, Matthew presents Jesus praying three times in Gethsemane, and the second rendering of Jesus's prayer contains the exact same words as the will petition: "Your will be done" (*genēthētō to thelēma sou*; 26:42).[27]

In the Lord's Prayer, we address the Father through our relationship with Jesus, his Son, and do so as the Father's adopted children. As we have seen, a defining marker of a child in the biblical tradition is obedience, and it is through obedience that a child shows love to the father. In Gethsemane, Jesus shows us the perfect obedience of the Father's Son. He consents to do the Father's will and carries it out perfectly in the events of his suffering and death.

This obedience of Christ, the Son, must become that of Christians, the Father's adopted children.[28] During his ministry, Jesus teaches, "Whoever does the will of my Father in heaven is my brother and sister and mother" (Matt. 12:50). To be a child of the Father is to

---

27. The Greek text of Matt. 6:10, "Your will be done," is *genēthētō to thelēma sou*.
28. Following here Martin and Rush, *When You Pray*, 41–42.

obey the Father's will. Jesus shows us perfect obedience to the Father as the Son, and in this regard, we are called to imitate his obedience to the Father's will in our lives. After Jesus's death and resurrection, it is a matter not simply of imitation but of participation. Through baptism, we become the Father's adopted children by sharing in the life of the risen Jesus, the Father's only Son. The life, and thus obedience, of Jesus comes to us.

We can thus discern a deep theological and spiritual connection between the kingdom and will petitions. Living under the Father's eschatological rule as king—that is, in the kingdom of God—involves total obedience to the Father's will. Obedience to the Father's will also marks the life of a child of the Father: Jesus, the Son of the Father, and Christians, who become the Father's adopted children by participating in the life of Jesus the Son. To live in the kingdom of God means to be a child of God, for both involve obedience to the Father's will.

The primary outlook of the kingdom and will petitions is public, communal, and eschatological. But there are also ways these petitions apply to the individual believer here and now. When one prays "Your kingdom come" and "Your will be done, on earth as it is in heaven" (Matt. 6:10), the first place where these realities need to happen is in one's own life.[29]

With these petitions, we pray for the grace to recognize and honor the Father's sovereignty in our lives by obeying his will. Conversely, we also pray for the grace to stop opposing and rebelling against his kingship by our sins.

This spirituality of faithful obedience is deeply embedded in the biblical tradition.[30] The petition "Your will be done" (Matt. 6:10) recalls the words of the people Israel at Mount Sinai: "Everything that the LORD has spoken we will do" (Exod. 19:8; cf. 24:3, 7). We see the same spiritual response in the words of the Virgin Mary to the angel Gabriel: "Let it happen to me according to your word"

29. Martin and Rush, *When You Pray*, 43.
30. Likewise argued in Martin and Wright, *Gospel of John*, 57, 60–61, 256.

(Luke 1:38, my translation; cf. John 2:5). Above all, this is the prayer of Jesus, who says to the Father, "Your will be done," and so brings about the salvation of the world (Matt. 26:42). It is the prayer of the faithful and obedient children of God.

Conclusion

The kingdom and the will petitions of the Lord's Prayer are thematically similar. Both are illumined by the biblical presentation of the Lord as the king. The kingdom petition in particular recalls God's promises in Scripture to act definitively as king in the end-time to put things right. Jesus himself teaches that the eschatological act of God as king is present in his own person and ministry, and at the same time, the reality of the kingdom also has aspects that are future. The definitive end-time saving act of God as king, Christians believe, has taken place in the death and resurrection of Jesus. The kingdom petition therefore asks the Father to reveal and realize fully in the world his kingly rule in Christ and so transform the world. This is something that will take place at Christ's parousia.

The will petition is an expansion of the kingdom petition. We pray for a specific component in the full realization of the kingdom of God: the securing of perfect goodness in the world and the complete removal of evil. That is, we pray that the Father's kingly will, which is now done perfectly in heaven, will be likewise realized in the world. We also pray to live now under the Father's kingly rule. That is, we pray for the obedience of Jesus, the Father's Son, to become our obedience. To do so is to live fully as the adopted children of "our Father in heaven" (Matt. 6:9).

5

Our Daily Bread

The "we" petitions make up the second group of petitions in the Lord's Prayer. Whereas in the "you" petitions we ask the Father to take action regarding something proper to himself, in the "we" petitions we ask the Father to take action regarding something pertaining to us human beings. These petitions use the first-person plural words "we," "us," and "our." Here we ask the Father to "give *us* . . . *our* daily bread" (Matt. 6:11, emphasis added; Luke 11:3), to "forgive *us our* sins for *we ourselves* forgive" (Luke 11:4, emphasis added; cf. Matt. 6:12), and to "not bring *us* to the time of trial, but rescue *us* from the evil one" (Matt. 6:13, emphasis added; cf. Luke 11:4).

The first "we" petition is the bread petition. Several interpretive challenges attend this petition. First, while Matthew and Luke give much of the same wording for this petition, there are some small yet significant differences. Second, these differences in wording give each version of the bread petition a somewhat different tone: Matthew's version has a stronger eschatological accent, while Luke's version attends more to the present. Third, a peculiar word is found in both versions of the prayer, and we do not really know what it means. It is the Greek word *epiousios*, which modifies "bread" and is translated as "daily" in the expression "our daily bread" (Matt. 6:11; Luke 11:3). As far as we know, this word is not found in any extant ancient Greek text apart from the Lord's Prayer. We can, however, make some educated guesses about its meaning based on etymology. The major options for understanding *epiousios* dovetail with the differences in tone of the two versions of the bread petition.

After examining these linguistic matters, we will consider both the present-oriented articulation of the bread petition in Luke and the more future-oriented articulation of it in Matthew. We will propose that with the bread petition, *we ask the Father to provide us with the sustenance we need to do his will in the present life and to live with him forever in the next.*[1]

The Language of the Bread Petition

The articulations of the bread petition in Matthew and Luke are for the most part identical.[2] They agree in asking the Father to provide "our daily bread" (*ton arton hēmōn ton epiousion*) "to us" (*hēmin*). The Greek word *artos* can mean "bread" or "loaves" (e.g., Matt. 4:3–4; 15:33–34; Luke 4:3–4; 14:17, 19), and it can also mean "food" more generally (e.g., Matt. 15:2, 26; Luke 7:33; 9:3).

There are two major linguistic differences between Matthew's version and Luke's version of this petition. First, there is the form of the verb meaning "give." Both Matthew and Luke use the common Greek verb meaning "give" (*didōmi*), but they give different forms of that verb. Matthew's version has the aorist active imperative form: *dos*. Luke's version, by contrast, uses the same verb but in the present imperative form: *didou*. Whereas an aorist imperative looks for an action to be completed on one occasion, a present imperative looks

---

1. I here follow Francis Martin, who in an unpublished text offers the following interpretive paraphrase of the bread petition: "Give us the bread we need for this life and the next." See also Martin and Rush, *When You Pray*, 43–48.
2. The Greek text for each version reads as follows: *ton arton hēmōn ton epiousion dos hēmin sēmeron* (Matt. 6:11); *ton arton hēmōn ton epiousion didou hēmin to kath' hēmeran* (Luke 11:3).

for an action to keep going on or to be repeated.[3] Luke's version of the petition asks the Father to keep giving bread or to do so many times over. Syntactically, Matthew's version envisions a single act of the Father, and Luke's version envisions the Father's continual action. Second, these differences in the verbs square with differences in adverbial expressions. Matthew modifies "give" with the word *sēmeron*, meaning "today" or, as the NRSV renders it, "this day" (6:11). The word emphasizes the present moment in time.[4] Luke employs a different expression to modify the imperative "give." He uses the prepositional phrase *kath' hēmeran*, which can mean "every day" or, as the NRSV translates it, "each day." This modifier complements Luke's use of the present imperative *didou* ("give"), which looks for the Father's continuing action. In other words, Matthew's version asks the Father to provide sustenance right now, and Luke's version has a wider horizon, asking the Father to keep providing sustenance for people each and every day.

Adding to the complexity is the aforementioned adjective *epiousios*, which modifies the noun "bread." Most translations, the NRSV included, render this word as "daily." It is often noted that Origen of Alexandria (d. ca. 240), a great early Christian biblical interpreter and philologist, was baffled by this word. He observed that the word *epiousios* "is not employed by any of the Greek writers, nor by philosophers, nor by individuals in common usage, but seems to have been formed by the evangelists."[5] Like Origen, we still do not know of any instance of this word in ancient Greek literature apart from the Lord's Prayer. The earliest Christians seemingly knew the sense of this word, but later readers do not.

Given the absence of comparative evidence, scholars normally make sense of the word by considering its etymology.[6] There are two

3. Béchard, *Syntax of New Testament Greek*, §3.1 (pp. 37–39).
4. Cf. Matt. 6:30; 11:23; 16:3; 21:28; 27:8, 19; 28:15.
5. Origen, *On Prayer* 27.7, quoted in Stewart-Sykes, *Tertullian, Cyprian, and Origen*, 178–79.
6. For discussion of the interpretive options, see "ἐπιούσιος," in BAGD, 296–97; Black, *Lord's Prayer*, 150–57; Bovon, *Luke 2*, 89–90; Brown, "Pater Noster," 239–40;

principal components to the word *epiousios*. The Greek word *epi* is a wide-ranging preposition that often means "on" or "upon." The *-ousios* component likely comes from one of two Greek words: one option is the verb *eimi* with the infinitive form *einai*, which means "to be"; or it might be the verb *eimi* with the infinitive form *ienai*, which means "to come."

In light of the philology, interpreters have offered a variety of proposals for the meaning of the *epiousios* bread. One set of options, building on the root meaning "to be," interprets the bread in terms of "being" or "existing." In this way, the bread concerns life in the present world. As Raymond Brown notes, it "could mean bread for the existing day" or the bread that we need "for existence."[7] So understood, the bread petition is asking the Father to provide us with the sustenance we need to live each day. This interpretation of *epiousios* informs the decision to translate it as "daily," and it pairs well with Luke's version of the petition.[8]

Another way to construe the etymology in terms of the verb "to be" is to understand it in terms of the heavenly or supernatural realm. It would align the etymology of *epiousios* with the idea that this bread comes from a domain that is spatially "upon" (*epi*) the realm of "being" (*ousia*).[9] Understood along these lines, the bread petition would be asking the Father to provide us with heavenly or supernatural sustenance.

Other interpretive options, building on the form of *eimi* that means "to come," are more oriented to the eschatological future. So understood, the *epiousios* bread would have the sense of "the bread for the coming day [or] for the future."[10] As we will discuss, Jesus

---

Davies and Allison, *Gospel according to Saint Matthew*, 1:607–8; Fitzmyer, *Gospel according to Luke*, 2:904–6; Luz, *Matthew 1–7*, 319–21.

7. Brown, "Pater Noster," 240.

8. The Old Latin text of Matt. 6:11 translates *epiousios* as *cottidianum* ("daily"). The Latin Vulgate likewise renders *epiousios* in Luke 11:3 as *cotidianum*.

9. Following Origen (*On Prayer* 27), the Latin Vulgate translates *epiousios* in Matt. 6:11 as *supersubtantialem*, interpreting the etymology as "upon" (Gk. *epi* ≈ Lat. *super*) and "being" or "substance" (Gk. *ousia* ≈ Lat. *substantia*).

10. Brown, "Pater Noster," 240. Scholars who favor this construal often call attention to a remark of Jerome (*Comm. Matt.* 6:11), who found *epiousios* rendered with

often speaks of the eschatological state of affairs, the kingdom of God, as a great banquet or dinner that God will host for his people. This idea of an eschatological banquet likewise appears in the Old Testament and in noncanonical Jewish writings near the time of Jesus. Taken in this light, the bread petition would be a request for the Father to provide us now with the food of the eschatological banquet. This interpretation would align with the eschatological tone of Matthew's version of the bread petition as well as with that of the other petitions that concern the full completion of the Father's plan at Christ's parousia.

The two versions of the bread petition in Matthew and Luke pull us in two somewhat different but ultimately complementary directions. Drawing on the analogy of looking at a precious stone from different sides (see chap. 1), we can think of Matthew and Luke as each drawing out different dimensions of Jesus's words. From one side, Jesus's instructions that we ask the Father to give us bread as sustenance for the present life cohere with his other teachings about the Father's generosity in providing what we need to live well (Matt. 6:31–33 // Luke 12:29–30). From another side, Jesus's request that we petition the Father for bread coheres with his teachings about the kingdom as a great banquet (Matt. 22:1–14) as well as with the aspects of his ministry that are present participations in the eschatological reality of the kingdom.

Exposition of the Bread Petition

Before delving into the substance of the bread petition, we should remind ourselves of some basic facts about the human condition. Human beings are, to use the expression of Alasdair MacIntyre, "dependent rational animals."[11] As composites of matter and spirit, we depend on various realities outside of ourselves in order to live

---

the Hebrew word *māḥār* ("tomorrow") in the apocryphal Gospel of the Hebrews. So Jerome, *Commentary on Matthew*, 88–89.

11. MacIntyre, *Dependent Rational Animals*.

in the world. These include, for instance, things like food and water, clothing, and shelter. Since human beings are by nature social and relational, we also depend in various ways on other people.[12] Most profoundly and comprehensively, we depend on God the Creator, who brings us (and all things) into existence and sustains us.[13]

Human beings are more than matter, and our needs exceed what the world can meet. For instance, we all have an innate desire for perfect and permanent happiness, a kind of happiness that nothing in the world can provide.[14] It is a yearning for the transcendent and the perfect. It is the human desire for God, and it is only God who can graciously satisfy this desire in us.[15] Not only do human beings depend on God for our existence at every moment, but we also rely on his graciousness to fulfill our deepest desires by bringing us to share in his eternal life.

Human beings are dependent creatures in manifold ways, and the two versions of the bread petition can be seen as speaking to both kinds of human needs, which we might call the natural and the supernatural. We need many things to sustain our life in this world, and even more importantly, we need a kind of supernatural sustenance to nourish our spiritual life for eternity.

First, when we pray "Give us our daily bread," we ask the Father to provide us with the sustenance we need to do his will in the present life. Throughout the Scriptures, we learn that the Lord is generous and compassionate, and he is the source of sustenance for his people. In particular, the Lord takes care of the poor and the needy, and we often hear that he provides food for the hungry.[16] Psalm 146:7 praises

---

12. So Aristotle, *Politics* 1.1253a.

13. This is a staple doctrine in the participatory metaphysics of creation, set forth by Thomas Aquinas. A (very) succinct statement of Aquinas's basic case is given in *Summa Theologiae* I, q. 3, a. 4. For secondary discussion, see Wright and Martin, *Encountering the Living God*, 130–40.

14. That happiness is the highest good for the sake of which human beings seek all other goods is argued by Aristotle in his *Nichomachean Ethics* 1.7 (1097ab).

15. As Augustine (*Confessions* 1.1.1) puts it: "You have made us for yourself, and our heart is restless until it rests in you" (Chadwick, 3).

16. In both testaments of the Christian Bible, the term for "bread" (Hb. *leḥem*; Gk. *artos*) can also mean "food" in a general sense.

the Lord, "who executes justice for the oppressed; who gives food to the hungry." Psalm 136:25 similarly declares that the Lord "gives food to all flesh." Psalm 145 praises the Lord for his goodness, generosity, and compassion and cites his providing food for the needy who approach him: "The eyes of all look to you, and you give them their food in due season" (v. 15).

One way the Lord provides for his people Israel is by giving them the land of Canaan. In Deuteronomy 8, Moses tells the Israelites, "[In the promised land] you may eat bread without scarcity. . . . You shall eat your fill and bless the LORD your God for the good land that he has given you" (vv. 9–10). The Israelites are to recognize that the promised land and its produce are gifts from God. They are to celebrate the (spring) harvest with a liturgical festival (Lev. 23:15–22; Deut. 16:9–12) and also offer the firstfruits of the harvest in thanksgiving to the Lord for this gift (Deut. 26:1–11).[17]

As faithful children of their covenantal Father, the people Israel are to imitate and put into practice the Lord's ways. Just as the Lord God takes care of the poor and the hungry, so should his people. In the Torah, the Israelites are instructed not to harvest the entirety of their fields or vineyards. Rather, they are to leave some of their crop at the edges of their field "for the poor and the alien" (Lev. 19:9–10; cf. 23:22). Deuteronomy 24 connects this practice of caring for the needy with the Israelites' own experience of being in need while in Egypt: "When you gather the grapes of your vineyard, do not glean what is left; it shall be for the alien, the orphan, and the widow. Remember that you were a slave in the land of Egypt; therefore I am commanding you to do this" (vv. 21–22).

Other passages similarly instruct God's people to take care of the hungry by sharing food with them. Proverbs 22:9 states, "Those who are generous are blessed, for they share their bread with the poor." In Isaiah 58, the Lord reprimands his people for neglecting righteous forms of living while performing religious observances. The prophet

17. This liturgical festival is known as the Festival of Weeks (or *Shavu'ot*) or Pentecost.

states, "Is not this the fast that I choose . . . ? Is it not to share your bread with the hungry, and bring the homeless poor into your house; when you see the naked, to cover them?" (vv. 6–7; cf. 58:10). The book of Tobit similarly presents us with the good man Tobit, who feeds the hungry (1:16–17) and instructs his son Tobias to do the same: "Give some of your food to the hungry, and some of your clothing to the naked" (4:16).

The Lord is the generous provider of sustenance for his people, and the poor and needy are important to him. God takes care of his people, especially the poor, and one way in which he does this is through intermediaries. The Lord provides food for the people Israel *through* the gift of the promised land. The Lord provides food for the hungry (in part) *through* his obedient people who imitate his generosity. The Lord instructs people to help the poor and hungry, and he reprimands them when they fail to do so.

Jesus amplifies this presentation in his teaching about the Father and his disciples' conduct. As discussed in chapter 2, the Father has a perfect and intimate knowledge of us and our needs, and he is eager to provide generously. The Father "knows what [we] need before [we] ask him" (Matt. 6:8), and he is the giver of good things. Jesus also tells us to trust in the Father's generosity, for he will provide us with what we need to live in a manner pleasing to him. In both Matthew and Luke, Jesus teaches against greed and the anxieties that the desire for worldly things can create (Matt. 6:19–34; Luke 12:22–34).[18] In this section of teaching, Jesus repeatedly tells his audience, "Do not worry" (Matt. 6:25, 31, 34; Luke 12:22, 25, 29). In this context, "worry" means that we become consumed with making our lives secure by acquiring and having things. Whereas the rich fool in the parable mistakenly thought his life was secure because of his possessions (Luke 12:16–21), Jesus tells his disciples, "Do not worry about your life, what you will eat, or about your body, what you will wear.

---

18. Luke 12:13–34 forms a coherent argumentative unit on this topic, which reflects a mode of rhetorical composition known as a "complete argument" or an "elaborated chreia." See Stegman, "Reading Luke 12:13–34," 328–52.

For life is more than food, and the body more than clothing" (Luke 12:22–23). Jesus notes that the Father provides food for the birds and covers the fields with flowers (Luke 12:24, 27–28). Jesus then teaches that the Father's care and concern for human beings far exceed his care and concern for other created things. If the Father takes care of the birds and the flowers of the field, which are "here today and gone tomorrow," then how much more will he provide for people: "Of how much more value are you than the birds!" (Luke 12:24).

The necessities of life are important, and as Jesus teaches, "your Father knows that you need them" (Luke 12:30). But instead of being consumed by the need to secure our lives by possessing things (which is really an illusion, a false sense of security), Jesus tells us to order our lives around the Father and to live under his kingly rule: "Strive first for the kingdom of God and his righteousness, and all these things will be given to you as well" (Matt. 6:33; cf. Luke 12:31). This does not mean that we should be unconcerned with the necessities of life, nor does it mean that the Father will spare us material hardships in the world and provide us with everything we request.[19] Rather, Jesus teaches us to make the Father the greatest good in our lives and to make living in a manner pleasing to him our highest priority: "Strive first for . . . his righteousness" (Matt. 6:33). If we do this, then the Father will provide us with all that we need to live in a manner pleasing to him. As W. D. Davies and Dale Allison write, "Jesus promises that the heavenly Father, through divine providence, will give his own what is truly necessary for them if they are to accomplish their God-given tasks."[20]

When we ask the Father to give us "our daily bread," we ask him to provide that which we need to sustain us in this life so that we can live in a manner pleasing to him. This interpretation resonates with Luke's version of the petition, which is more oriented to day-to-day living in the present world.

Another angle on this petition comes to light in the instructions Jesus gives to the twelve apostles and the seventy disciples when he

19. Davies and Allison, *Gospel according to Saint Matthew*, 1:664.
20. Davies and Allison, *Gospel according to Saint Matthew*, 1:664.

sends them out on a mission (Luke 9:1–6; 10:1–12). Jesus dispatches the Twelve "to proclaim the kingdom of God and to heal" (9:2), and he tells them, "Take nothing for your journey, no staff, nor bag, nor bread, nor money" (9:3). They are doing the Father's work, and they are to rely on others to provide for their needs (9:4). When Jesus sends out the seventy disciples, he similarly tells them to rely on the generosity of others: "Whenever you enter a town and its people welcome you, eat what is set before you" (10:8). Implied here is the Father's action to meet their needs through the generosity of others. In the Scriptures, God provided food for people through intermediaries such as the promised land and his faithful people, and we can see the same thing here: the Father can provide us with "our daily bread" through generous people.

When we take the bread petition in this light, we can also detect an implicit summons to be generous ourselves. Recall that in the Old Testament, Israel is called to imitate the goodness and generosity of God by taking care of those among them in need. Jesus summons his disciples to do the same. Insofar as we respond to Jesus's call to help generously those in need, we are opening ourselves to being the means by which the Father provides others with their "daily bread." Jesus instructs us to give alms to the poor (Matt. 6:2–4; 19:21) and to provide practical assistance to the needy. In Matthew's famous scene of the last judgment, the enthroned Jesus admits to the kingdom of heaven those who fed the hungry, welcomed the stranger, sated the thirsty, gave clothes to the naked, took care of the sick, and visited the imprisoned (25:34–36)—and those who did not do so are excluded from the kingdom of heaven (25:41–46). When we ask the Father to give us "our daily bread," we can also hear in Jesus's words a subtle call to be generous and so be available as the means by which the Father answers this prayer in the lives of others.

Second, when we pray "Give us our daily bread," we also ask the Father to provide us with the sustenance we need to live with him forever in the next life. The bread petition can be interpreted as having an eschatological or transcendent tone. As discussed above, the term *epiousios*, which modifies "bread," could possibly mean "the bread that is to come" or even "the supernatural bread." If taken in this light, the petition can be understood as asking the Father to give to us now the bread of the eschatological future or the bread of heaven—that is, the food of the kingdom of God.

Interpretations of the bread petition as a request for eschatological and/or heavenly food find support from elements in the Old Testament, in Jewish writings near the time of Jesus, and in the teaching of Jesus himself. Important for our purposes are two key biblical episodes that speak of God providing food for his people: the manna episode and the description of the eschatological banquet.

The most famous time in the Old Testament when God gives bread to his people is when he provides them with manna in the wilderness. While in the wilderness after leaving Egypt, the Israelites complain about not having food to eat. In response, the Lord tells Moses, "I am going to rain bread from heaven for you, and each day the people shall go out and gather enough for that day" (Exod. 16:4). The next day, when the Israelites see the manna on the ground and do not know what it is, Moses explains, "It is the bread that the LORD has given you to eat" (16:15). By feeding Israel with the manna, the Lord reveals himself to be Israel's God, who sustains and provides for them (16:12).

In later texts and traditions, the manna came to be interpreted as having transcendent and eschatological dimensions.[21] For instance, Psalm 78 describes the manna as "bread from heaven" (cf. Exod. 16:4) and interprets it as heavenly food. The text says that the Lord "opened the doors of heaven; he rained down on them manna to eat, and gave them the grain of heaven" (Ps. 78:23–24). The psalmist goes on to identify the manna as the food of the angels: "Mortals ate of the bread of angels; he sent them food in abundance" (78:25). This identification of the manna as angelic food continues in the Wisdom of Solomon. In Wisdom 16, the author speaks of the manna as the angels' food, which God provided freely to Israel: "You gave your

21. See Kugel, *Bible as It Was*, 358–62.

people food of angels, and without their toil you supplied them from heaven with bread ready to eat" (v. 20). The text goes on to describe the otherworldly property of the manna: it tasted like whatever the one eating wanted it to be (16:21).[22]

The manna also appears in Jewish and Christian anticipations of the eschatological age. The book of Revelation mentions the manna as an eschatological gift. In the letter to the church at Pergamum, the glorified Jesus promises some of "the hidden manna" as a reward to every Christian who "conquers" (Rev. 2:17). That is, Jesus will provide this heavenly sustenance as a reward to those who remain faithful to him even unto death. In a first-century Jewish apocalyptic writing called 2 Baruch, there is a passage that speaks of a time at the end of days when the messiah will appear after a time of great distress and defeat his monstrous enemies (26:1–30:5). The messiah's victory will usher in a time of superabundance and prosperity when all will have their fill (29:4–6). It is also during the messianic age that God will once again send manna from heaven as food for the blessed: "It will happen at that time that the treasury of manna will come down again from on high, and they will eat of it in those years because these are they who will have arrived at the consummation of time" (29:8).[23]

This description in 2 Baruch 29 of the eschatological age when God will provide for his people a superabundance of food (including the manna) is an example of another theme in ancient Jewish and Christian literature: the eschatological banquet. When biblical prophets speak of the eschatological state of affairs that God will bring about, they often describe it in terms of a superabundance of food and wine (e.g., Jer. 31:10–14; Joel 4:18; Amos 9:11–15). The eschatological banquet is a particular expression of this theme.

The first place where the eschatological banquet as such appears is in Isaiah 25. Here, the great eschatological banquet is a part of the

---

22. Kugel (*Bible as It Was*, 360–61) gives examples from other ancient Jewish and Christian readers who exemplified this line of interpretation.
23. Citations of 2 Baruch taken from Charlesworth, *Old Testament Pseudepigrapha*, vol. 1.

larger vision of God's end-time saving action, wherein he puts down his opponents and reigns as king from Mount Zion (Isa. 24:23). The Lord's eschatological victory and kingly reign bring about a transformation of the world.[24] With the Lord having won his kingly victory, the announcement goes out of a great feast hosted by the Lord, the king, on Mount Zion: "On this mountain the LORD of hosts will make for all peoples a feast of rich food, a feast of well-aged wines, of rich food filled with marrow, of well-aged wines strained clear" (Isa. 25:6). The Lord holds this sumptuous dinner party "for all peoples" (25:6). This detail signals that the eschatological age is a permanent state of peace and reconciliation among peoples.[25] All come together at this great feast under the kingly rule of the Lord, who provides them with all they need. This theme of the eschatological banquet was variously developed in ancient Jewish and Christian circles.[26]

The Gospels show that Jesus used the theme of the eschatological banquet in his ministry. On many occasions, Jesus compares the kingdom of God to a banquet or dinner feast. When praising the faith of a Roman centurion, Jesus hints at the welcoming of gentiles into the eschatological feast that is the kingdom: "Many will come from east and west and will eat with Abraham and Isaac and Jacob in the kingdom of heaven" (Matt 8:11; cf. Luke 13:29). Jesus compares the kingdom of heaven to a feast in the parable of the wedding banquet (Matt. 22:1–14 // Luke 14:15–24) and the parable of the bridesmaids (Matt. 25:1–13). In Luke's account of the Last Supper, Jesus imparts the kingdom of God to the twelve apostles and says to them, "You may eat and drink at my table in my kingdom, and you will sit on thrones judging the twelve tribes of Israel" (22:30). Also at the Last

24. Included in the eschatological transformation of the world are the following: the Lord will destroy death (Isa. 25:7–8); he "will wipe away the tears from all faces" (25:8); and he will forgive his people who will in turn praise him (25:8–10).
25. Blenkinsopp, *Isaiah 1–39*, 359–60; Tucker, *Book of Isaiah 1–39*, 216.
26. Examples include 1 En. 25:4–6; 60:24; 62:13–14; 1QSa 2:11–20; 4 Ezra 6:49–52; 2 Bar. 29:1–8. For discussion of these and other examples, see Moore, *Judaism in the First Centuries*, 2:363–65; Pitre, *Jesus and the Last Supper*, 448–58; Smith, "Messianic Banquet," 4:788–91.

Supper, Jesus voices his confident expectation that the Father will vindicate him after his death by saying that he will once again eat and drink in the kingdom (Matt. 26:29; Luke 22:16, 18). The banquet motif also informs Jesus's practice of table fellowship. In his ministry, Jesus shared meals with his disciples and "tax-collectors and sinners" (Matt. 9:11; cf. Luke 15:1–2), and all who would welcome him. Taken in light of his likening of the kingdom to a dinner, these meals hosted by Jesus are illuminated as anticipated participations in the eschatological banquet of the kingdom of God. As Joachim Jeremias writes, "Every meal with Jesus was a salvation meal, an anticipation of the final feast. At each meal he was the host, as he would be at the consummation."[27]

With the Lord's provision of manna and these end-time meals in view, the bread petition can be interpreted as a request for the Father to provide us with the food of his eschatological kingdom, the sustenance of eternal life. We have seen that Jesus's teaching about the kingdom of God exhibits a tension between present and future, immanence and transcendence. The kingdom of God is in some respects present in Jesus and his ministry, and in other respects, it is something future. As Jesus taught that the eschatological realities of the kingdom were in some ways genuinely present in him and his ministry, so too are there components of his ministry that suggest that Jesus welcomes people in some ways to share now in the banquet of the eschatological kingdom.[28] Of particular interest in this regard are the only two instances in the Gospels where Jesus himself is said to *give bread* to people.

The first instance is the feeding miracle when Jesus multiplies loaves and fish to feed a great crowd.[29] The Gospel accounts of this

---

27. Jeremias, *New Testament Theology*, 200.

28. Such thinking is comparable in some ways (and different in others) to the Essenes of Qumran who regarded their community meals as present participations in the eschatological banquet. See 1QS 6; 1QSa 2:11–20; and for discussion, Schiffman, *Reclaiming the Dead Sea Scrolls*, 334–39.

29. This analysis of the feeding miracle is indebted to de la Potterie, "Multiplication of the Loaves," 499–516.

episode are richly textured and contain allusions to a variety of biblical topics.[30] Important for our purposes are the connections between the feeding miracle and the manna. For one, there is the location of the feeding miracle. In Matthew and Luke, it occurs in "a deserted place" (Matt. 14:15 // Luke 9:12). The descriptor of the location as "deserted" (*erēmos*) is the same term used throughout the LXX for "the wilderness" where the Israelites dwelled before entering the promised land. In particular, Exodus 16 specifies that "the wilderness" is where the Lord fed the Israelites with the manna (vv. 14, 32 LXX).

A second set of allusions to the manna tradition concerns the crowd. In the Gospels, the crowds Jesus feeds are massive in size: over five thousand people (Matt. 14:21; 15:38; Luke 9:14). Similarly, the exodus narrative depicts the Israelite group who left Egypt and were fed by the manna as numbering in the hundreds of thousands (Exod. 12:37). In both the Gospels and Exodus, the crowds are fed with bread in the wilderness because they do not have any food to eat (Exod. 16:3; Matt. 14:15; 15:32; Luke 9:12). There is also the detail in the feeding miracle that Jesus had the crowds "sit down in groups of about fifty each" (Luke 9:14).[31] This seating arrangement of people in sets of fifties might be a further allusion to the Israelites in the wilderness, who were grouped in sets of fifties when put under judges appointed by Moses (Exod. 18:21, 25; Deut. 1:15).[32]

A third set of connections appears in the feeding miracle. When Jesus performs this miracle, he "gives" (*didōmi*) to his disciples and the crowds "loaves of bread" (*artos*) to eat.[33] When Exodus 16 LXX presents the manna episode, it states that the Lord "gives" (*didōmi*) to the Israelites "bread" (*artos*) to eat.[34] The Gospel accounts of Jesus

---

30. These include, for instance, the feeding miracle worked by Elisha the prophet (2 Kings 4:42–44) and the presentation of the Lord as a shepherd who feeds his people and has them "sit down on the grass" (Matt. 14:19; cf. Ps. 23:2).

31. This detail is more pronounced in Mark 6:39–40.

32. Cf. de la Potterie, "Multiplication of the Loaves," 504–5.

33. Forms of these two Greek words appear in Matt. 14:19; 15:36; Luke 9:16.

34. This pairing of words appears in Exod. 16:8, 15, 29 LXX.

giving bread to the crowds thus echo the descriptions in Exodus 16 LXX of the Lord giving bread to the Israelites.

The feeding miracle thus recalls the gift of manna in the wilderness. But the feeding miracle also looks forward to the eschatological future. Biblical prophets often spoke of the eschatological age as a time of a great superabundance of food. In the feeding miracle, Jesus provides a superabundance of food. Not only does he multiply a few loaves and fish so that a massive crowd can all eat their fill, but there is also a huge amount of bread left over (Matt. 14:20–21 // Luke 9:17). Moreover, there was a Jewish hope for the return of the manna at the eschatological banquet in the messianic age (2 Bar. 29:8). Luke situates the feeding miracle in the context of Jesus teaching "about the kingdom of God" and healing the sick—two acts that are present instantiations of the kingdom (Luke 9:11; cf. Matt. 14:14). When Jesus performs a miracle that recalls the manna, we can see in this event the eschatological banquet of the kingdom becoming present in a real, though limited, way. Like Jesus's practice of table fellowship, the feeding miracle is an anticipated participation in the eschatological banquet of the kingdom of God.[35]

The only other place in the Gospels where Jesus "gives bread" to people is the institution of the Eucharist at the Last Supper. The Gospels show that the feeding miracle and the Eucharist are literarily and theologically related. These associations point to the Eucharist as another mode in which the eschatological realities of the kingdom become present to people as their food.

Jesus performs similar gestures with the bread at both the feeding miracle and the Last Supper. At the feeding miracle, "taking the five loaves and the two fish, [Jesus] looked up to heaven, and blessed and broke the loaves, and gave them to the disciples" (Matt. 14:19; cf. Luke 9:16). Jesus performs these same gestures—he takes, blesses, breaks, and gives bread—at the Last Supper: "While they were eating, Jesus took a loaf of bread, and after blessing it he broke it, [and] gave it to the disciples" (Matt. 26:26; cf. Luke 22:19).

---

35. So too Davies and Allison, *Gospel according to Saint Matthew*, 1:609.

Both the feeding miracle and the Eucharist align Jesus's community with the exodus community. In the feeding miracle, the crowd in the miracle story is very sympathetic to Jesus: they seek him out and stay with him until evening as he teaches and heals. This crowd whom Jesus feeds with bread in the wilderness is aligned with the Israelites whom the Lord feeds with manna in the wilderness. The Last Supper bears numerous associations with the exodus tradition, not least of which its character as a Passover(-like) meal.[36] At the Last Supper, Jesus identifies the Eucharistic cup with the formation of a "covenant" community. Matthew and Mark bring out in Jesus's words an allusion to the formation of the Sinai covenant (Exod. 24:8; cf. Matt. 26:28; Mark 14:24), whereas Luke and Paul highlight an association with the eschatological new covenant, prophesied by Jeremiah and developed by Ezekiel (Jer. 31:31–34; Ezek. 36:24–28; cf. Luke 22:20; 1 Cor. 11:25).[37] In both cases, Jesus provides food to those who attach themselves to him and does so in settings that recall the exodus (and implicitly look forward to the eschatological new exodus).

Both the feeding miracle and the Eucharist are instances in which transcendent, eschatological realities are given to people in their present moment. Our grasp of the eschatological dimensions of the Eucharist can be enhanced by expanding our field of vision to other parts of the New Testament canon, especially Paul and John. When recounting Jesus's institution of the Eucharist in connection with the Corinthians' practice, Paul speaks of the Eucharist as being celebrated in anticipation of Jesus's parousia: "As often as you eat this bread and drink the cup, you proclaim the Lord's death until he comes" (1 Cor. 11:26). Christians look forward to the parousia in their celebration of the Eucharist. At the same time, they also enjoy communion with Christ in the present moment when they consume his Eucharistic

36. On the exodus connections of the Last Supper, see the discussion in Jeremias, *Eucharistic Words of Jesus*, esp. chaps. 1, 5; Pitre, *Jesus and the Last Supper*, chaps. 2–3, 5.
37. Helpfully put in Ratzinger (Pope Benedict XVI), *Jesus of Nazareth Part Two*, 126–27.

body and blood. Using the same Greek word he used in 1 Corinthians 1:9 for the church's union with the risen Jesus (*koinōnia*), Paul asks rhetorically, "The cup of blessing that we bless, is it not a sharing [or communion; *koinōnia*] in the blood of Christ? The bread that we break, is it not a sharing [*koinōnia*] in the body of Christ?" (1 Cor. 10:16). Communion with the risen Jesus, which the Corinthians now possess and which constitutes their share in Christ's eschatological life and victory at the resurrection (1 Cor. 15:22, 57–58), is fostered and deepened by their consuming of Christ's body in the Eucharist. In the Fourth Gospel's bread of life discourse (which develops the association between Jesus and the manna), there is a similar picture of the present realization of eschatological realities in the Eucharist. Jesus teaches that those who consume his Eucharistic body and blood have eternal life and a share in the end-time resurrection to life (John 6:54, 58). These future realities are a present possession because the Eucharist is communion with Jesus in the present moment: "Those who eat my flesh and drink my blood abide in me, and I in them" (John 6:56).

Taken in this context, the Eucharist comes to light as a present sharing in transcendent, eschatological realities. If the kingdom of God can be interpreted (canonically) as our becoming children of the Father by participating in the life of the Son, then our consuming of Christ's Eucharistic body and blood can be reckoned as the food of the kingdom. This is because our consumption of the Eucharistic food is, as Paul writes, "communion" with the risen Jesus in the present moment (1 Cor. 10:16).

Conclusion

The bread petition reminds us that we are dependent creatures who are in need of so many things outside of ourselves in order to live. This applies to our natural life in this world and our supernatural life in the next. The two versions of the bread petition speak to both sets of needs.

When we pray the bread petition, we are asking the Father to provide us with all that we need to live in a manner pleasing to him in this life. The Father knows our nature and our needs, and Jesus teaches us to have confidence in his goodness and generosity. Implicitly, Jesus also instructs us to be generous to others in need and thus make ourselves available to be the means through whom the Father may answer this prayer in the lives of others.

The bread petition also asks the Father to provide us with the sustenance we need to live with him forever in the next life. We ask the Father to provide us with the sustenance of his kingdom, the food of the eschatological banquet. Just as Jesus spoke of the kingdom as genuinely present in him and his ministry, so too are there ways Jesus offers people a present share in the eschatological food of the kingdom. He did this in one way during his ministry in his practice of table fellowship and feeding miracles. He continues to provide us with heavenly, eschatological sustenance in the Eucharist.

6

Forgive Us as We Forgive

The next "we" petition is the forgiveness petition, which appears in both Matthew and Luke. Both versions of this petition have the same two-clause structure. There is a main clause (i.e., the petition proper) in which we ask the Father to forgive us for the sins we have committed. Following upon the petition proper is a subordinate clause in which we connect the forgiveness that we ask the Father to show us with the forgiveness that we extend to those who wrong us.

Sin and forgiveness are prominent topics in the Gospel accounts of Jesus's ministry. Helpful for our purposes are the ways Jesus illustrates the nature of sin and forgiveness through parables in Matthew and Luke. We will unpack the substance of the forgiveness petition by way of certain parables that display in story form what Jesus teaches us in this petition. In the forgiveness petition, *we repent of our sins and ask the Father to forgive us, confident in his goodness. We also commit ourselves to imitate his ways of goodness and forgiveness in our dealings with others, for we ask the Father to forgive us in light of our forgiving those who wrong us.*

The Language of the Forgiveness Petition

Both versions of the forgiveness petition feature a Semitic idiom for talking about sin. The biblical writings employ a range of images to capture different aspects of the reality of sin and its consequences. These have been masterfully explored by Gary Anderson in his book *Sin: A History*. Anderson explains that the predominant image for sin in much of the Old Testament is that of a burden or weight that a person carries.[1] This image of sin as a burden informs, for instance, the Yom Kippur liturgy. Here, the high priest ritually places the sins of the Israelite community on the scapegoat, and when it is driven out into the wilderness, the scapegoat carries away the people's sins (Lev. 16:21–22).[2] This example also illustrates that each metaphor for sin has a correlate metaphor for forgiveness. In this case, when God forgives sin, the burden is lifted off or carried away.[3]

During the Persian period, the major image for sin in biblical and other ancient Jewish writings changes from a burden to an economic debt.[4] This is due, Anderson argues, to the growing use of Aramaic (the language of the Persian Empire) and the Jewish use of the Aramaic term for an economic debt (*ḥōb*) to designate sin.[5] It should not be surprising that Jesus, a Jewish man of the later Second Temple period and whose spoken language was Aramaic, would use the economic metaphor of debt to designate sin in the Lord's Prayer. Matthew's version of the Lord's Prayer uses only the language of "debts" and "debtors" (6:12). Luke, however, interprets the meaning of the Semitic idiom for his audience (who probably would not understand it) by varying his terms for wrongdoings: "Forgive us our sins" and "We ourselves forgive everyone indebted to us" (11:4).

Matthew's version of the forgiveness petition reads, "And forgive us our debts, as we also have forgiven our debtors" (6:12).[6] The forms of the verb "forgive" in the petition proper and the subordinate clause are in two different tenses. In the petition proper, the Greek verb for

---

1. G. Anderson, *Sin*, 15–26.
2. G. Anderson, *Sin*, 22–23.
3. G. Anderson, *Sin*, 4.
4. G. Anderson, *Sin*, 27–39.
5. G. Anderson, *Sin*, 27.
6. The Greek text of Matt. 6:12 reads as follows: *kai aphes hēmin ta opheilēmata hēmōn, hōs kai hēmeis aphēkamen tois opheiletais hēmōn.*

"forgive" (*aphes*) is an aorist imperative, which looks for a particular occasion when the Father will pardon us. In the subordinate clause ("as we also have forgiven . . ."), the verb "forgiven" (*aphēkamen*) is in the perfect tense. In Greek, the perfect tense connotes an action that has been completed in the past and has effects lasting into the present.[7] Taken together, these verbs point us to a time when we ask the Father to forgive us in light of our having previously forgiven those who have wronged us. The language of the petition can accommodate any particular moment when we ask the Father for pardon. But the combination of verbs in the aorist and perfect tenses likely points in particular to the moment of our standing before the judgment seat of God. We pray that at that moment, the Father will forgive us of our sins in light of our having forgiven those who have wronged us throughout our lives.

A similar picture emerges from Luke's version of the forgiveness petition: "And forgive us our sins, for we ourselves forgive everyone indebted to us" (11:4).[8] In the petition proper, Luke uses the same aorist imperative as Matthew for "forgive" (*aphes*). But unlike Matthew's wording, Luke's subordinate clause features the verb for "forgive" in the present tense: "For we ourselves forgive [*aphiomen*] everyone indebted to us" (11:4). Similar to his version of the bread petition, Luke's version of the forgiveness petition encompasses more plainly not only the moment of final judgment but also any moment when we ask the Father to forgive us.[9]

The relation between the two clauses is complex in part because Matthew and Luke use different conjunctions to connect the two clauses of the petition. In 6:12, Matthew uses the Greek word *hōs* ("like, as"), a term that expresses a relation and comparison between God's forgiving us and our forgiving others: "As we also have forgiven our debtors." In 11:4, Luke uses the Greek conjunction *gar* ("for"),

7. The perfect tense "denotes the *continuance* of *completed action*" (Blass, Debrunner, and Funk, *Greek Grammar*, §340 [p. 175]).

8. The Greek text of Luke 11:4 reads as follows: *kai aphes hēmin tas hamartias hēmōn, kai gar autoi aphiomen panti opheilonti hemin.*

9. Fitzmyer, *Gospel according to Luke*, 2:906.

which has a causal sense: "For we ourselves forgive everyone indebted to us." We will discuss this matter more below, but for the moment, we should register that both versions of the prayer present the subordinate clause as a kind of condition established by God. In both cases, we ask the Father to forgive us in light of how we forgive (or refuse to forgive) those who wrong us.

Jesus teaches that the forgiveness of sins and reconciliation with the Father are available to all people through him. The Gospels provide much content with which we can explore the theological substance of this petition. Particularly helpful in this regard are two of Jesus's parables: Luke's parable of the prodigal son (15:11–32) and Matthew's parable of the unforgiving servant (18:23–35). These two parables provide a dramatic display of that which is entailed by the forgiveness petition.

Exposition of the Forgiveness Petition

First, when we pray the forgiveness petition, we repent of our sins and ask the Father to forgive us with confidence in his goodness. Throughout the Scriptures, the Lord summons people to repent of their sins, and for his part, the Lord promises to forgive them (e.g., Deut. 4:29–31; 30:1–3; Jer. 3:12–14). The prophet Hosea calls out, "Return, O Israel, to the LORD your God, for you have stumbled because of your iniquity" (Hosea 14:1). And the Lord says, "I will heal their disloyalty; I will love them freely, for my anger has turned from them" (14:4).

The Scriptures repeatedly affirm that the Lord, the God of Israel, is forgiving and compassionate. When Moses ascends Mount Sinai to receive a new set of tablets of the commandments, after the first set had been broken in the golden calf incident, the Lord pronounces his name and declares the following: "The LORD, the LORD, a God merciful and gracious, slow to anger, and abounding in steadfast love and faithfulness, keeping steadfast love for the thousandth generation, forgiving iniquity and transgression and sin, yet by no means clearing the guilty, but visiting the iniquity of the parents upon the children and the children's children, to the third and the fourth generation" (Exod. 34:6–7). The Lord reveals himself here to be "merciful and gracious," full of "steadfast love," and "forgiving iniquity and transgression and sin." The Lord is also just and holds the guilty to account for their wrongdoing. But whereas the Lord's punishment for sins reaches to three or four generations, his love far exceeds this, reaching to the thousandth generation.

The prophet Micah declares that not only is the Lord merciful, but he even rejoices to forgive sins: "Who is a God like you, pardoning iniquity and passing over the transgression of the remnant of your possession? He does not retain his anger forever, because he delights in showing clemency" (7:18). Echoing Exodus 34, the psalmist praises the Lord for his love and mercy: "For you, O Lord, are good and forgiving, abounding in steadfast love to all who call on you" (Ps. 86:5; cf. 86:15). Elsewhere, the psalmist declares, "If you, O LORD, should mark iniquities, Lord, who could stand? But there is forgiveness with you, so that you may be revered" (130:3–4). Pertinent for the forgiveness petition of the Lord's Prayer is Psalm 103 (a text discussed previously with regard to the fatherhood of God in the Old Testament). This psalm likens the Lord's compassionate mercy for his people to a father's compassionate mercy for his children: "As a father has compassion for his children, so the LORD has compassion for those who fear him" (v. 13).[10]

In the Gospels, Jesus issues a call to repent and receive him and his message in faith (Matt. 3:2; 4:17; Luke 13:1–5). Jesus shows a special concern for sinners, deliberately seeking them out and welcoming them into his company. When challenged about his practice of sharing fellowship meals with sinners, Jesus responds to his critics, "Those who are well have no need of a physician, but those who are sick; I

---

10. This thinking is likewise present in the sixth benediction of the Amidah: "Forgive us, our Father, for we have sinned against thee, Erase and blot out our transgressions from before thine eyes, For thou art abundantly compassionate." Cited from Heinemann and Petuchowski, *Literature of the Synagogue*, 34.

have come to call not the righteous but sinners to repentance" (Luke 5:31–32; cf. Matt. 9:13; Mark 2:17). Jesus himself claims the divine authority to forgive people's sins in light of their response to him (e.g., Matt. 9:1–8 parr.; Luke 7:47–49).

Luke's Gospel places great emphasis on Jesus as a bringer of forgiveness and reconciliation. Perhaps no other episode in the Gospels shows in such dramatic fashion the character of sin, repentance, and the Father's eager forgiveness—all of which are involved in the forgiveness petition—as the parable of the prodigal son (15:11–32). Without rehearsing the parable in its entirety, we will highlight three of the parable's major elements that can help us understand better the petition "Father . . . forgive us our sins" (11:2, 4).

First, the parable teaches us about the reality of our sins through the conduct of both sons. The actions of the younger son show us that when we sin, we are personally offending God and rejecting him as our Father. The younger son opens with a request, "Father, give me the share of the property that will belong to me" (Luke 15:12). Some have argued that the son's request, though unconventional, is not necessarily out of line.[11] Or it may be that, as Kenneth Bailey has argued from a cultural point of view, for the younger son to ask for such control over his part of the inheritance while his father is still alive is effectively wishing that his father would die.[12] Either way, the father grants the younger son's unconventional, if not outright insulting, request (15:12). The younger son then does a number of things that break down relationships as well as his own self. He liquidates his inheritance, leaves the family, goes far away from his father, and spends all his money in self-serving ways.[13] But after he runs out of money and famine hits, the younger son tries to survive

---

11. Bovon, *Luke 2*, 424; Green, *Gospel of Luke*, 580. In terms of general background, Joachim Jeremias discusses the legal structures wherein a father's property could come to a son, both before and after the father's death. See Jeremias, *Parables of Jesus*, 128–29.

12. Bailey, *Cross and the Prodigal*, 30–31.

13. The expression "gathered all he had" (Luke 15:13) can mean to sell off all the property for cash. So Jeremias, *Parables of Jesus*, 129; see "συνάγω," in BAGD, 782.

by doing the work of a swineherd—a job that would be especially shameful to Jewish sensibilities. At this point, the younger son has hit rock bottom, for even the pigs are in a better state than he is: the pigs have something to eat, but "no one gave him anything" (15:16).[14]

At the end of the parable, the older son shows how self-righteousness, self-interest, and entitlement can blind us to the Father's goodness and our own need to repent. The older son does not welcome his brother back home, and he resents that his father has done so. He also refuses his father's pleading for him to receive his brother back.[15] The older son is completely caught up in himself and his own self-righteousness. His words to his father reveal his self-interest and sense of entitlement: "For all these years *I* have been working like a slave for you, and *I* have never disobeyed your command; yet you have never given *me* even a young goat so that *I* might celebrate with *my* friends" (Luke 15:29, emphasis added). As we have seen, in the biblical tradition, a son is supposed to learn from, imitate, and obey his father. The older son, in his refusal to forgive his brother and welcome him home, shows that he too is far from his father's ways, even though he never physically left home. The older son's actions illustrate how self-righteousness and self-absorption not only blind the mind but can also impair the will. They can keep us from loving and forgiving others as the Father does. The older son shows us a more subtle but very real way in which people (especially the pious) can fail to honor and imitate the ways of our loving Father.

Through our sins, we also destroy ourselves and our relationships with others. Through his actions at the start of the parable, the younger son severely damages his relationship with the father (and implicitly with his older brother). At the end of the parable, the older

14. Bailey, *Cross and the Prodigal*, 46. Joel B. Green (*Gospel of Luke*, 580–81) writes, the younger son "had little recourse but to locate himself in a situation wherein he has not only shamed his father (cf. Prov. 8:27) but has plummeted from his status as the son of a large landowner to that of the 'unclean and degraded,' for whom even the life of a day laborer would be preferable."

15. The older son does not even acknowledge his relationship with his younger brother, referring to him as "this son of yours" (Luke 15:30).

son shames his father by refusing to enter the feast, and he does not even recognize his younger brother as his sibling anymore.[16] The sins of the two sons create all kinds of dysfunction and wounds in the interpersonal relationships depicted in the parable.

On two occasions, the father speaks of his younger son as having been dead and then returned to life when he came home: "This son of mine was dead and is alive again" (Luke 15:24; cf. 15:32). With these words, the father identifies the miserable state into which the younger son descended by his bad actions as a kind of death.[17] The father's words remind us that our sins not only bring us into misery and shame but can even destroy us spiritually. At the same time, our Father is so good, loving, and compassionate that he can bring us out from this state of shame and spiritual death by forgiving us. When we pray the forgiveness petition, we are asking the Father to do this very thing.

The parable of the prodigal son also teaches us about repentance, a second important element to draw out from this parable and bring to bear on the forgiveness petition. When we make the request of the Father, we acknowledge that we have sinned, and we ask for pardon—that is, we are repenting. We especially see the dynamics of repentance in the actions of the younger son.

The younger son's repentance begins when he recognizes the misery of his present state.[18] This prompts him to go home to his father (Luke 15:18). He does this, in a sense, because he knows his father's goodness in light of his father's previous actions. The younger son knows that his father provides well for his laborers, and so, in a way, the father's goodness moves the younger son to go home (15:17). As he works out what he will say to his father, the younger son begins by humbly acknowledging his relationship with his father,

16. On the older son's refusal to enter the feast as a cultural shaming of the father, see Bailey, *Cross and the Prodigal*, 69.
17. The association of sin and death appears in a variety of scriptural texts: Wis. 2:23–24; Rom. 5:12–14, 21; 1 Cor. 15:56; James 1:15.
18. François Bovon (*Luke 2*, 426) notes that the expression "he came to himself" (Luke 15:17) has purchase in ancient discussions of conversion.

for he opens with the address "Father" (15:18). This is a striking contrast with the later words of the older son, who never even addresses his father but instead begins by giving him an order: "Listen!" (15:29).

The younger son then confesses his wrongdoing and admits his fault: "I have sinned against heaven and before you" (Luke 15:18, 21). Through his actions, the younger son has offended both God and his earthly father, those to whom the son owes obedience and honor.[19] Next, the younger son acknowledges that his actions have damaged his relationship and standing with his father: "I am no longer worthy to be called your son" (15:19). Last, without a leg to stand on, he throws himself on his father's mercy and asks for treatment that would allow him to make things right: "Treat me like one of your hired hands" (15:19).

The younger son shows us important elements of repentance. He acknowledges his relationship with the father and does so in deference and humility. The younger son goes to his father, to whom he confesses his sin and his fault. He then throws himself on his father's mercy, trusting in his goodness and seeking a way to make things right.

Third, the parable teaches us about the unimaginable depth of the Father's mercy, compassion, and goodness. The father's conduct toward both of his sons is unconventional and unexpected. He publicly sprints to meet his younger son, who is on his way home (Luke 15:20), and he takes his younger son back with extraordinary generosity. Later, the father leaves in the middle of the dinner feast to go out to his older son (15:28). In both cases, Bailey argues, the father would incur public shame, but he does so out of his loving concern for his sons.[20] The parable thus shows us the lengths to which the Father will go to seek us out, urge us to come home to him, and show us his loving-kindness.

19. Bovon (*Luke 2*, 427) writes, "Without specifying what his sin was, the younger son realized that he had at the same time violated the order established by God and had been detrimental to his father's interests."
20. So Bailey, *Cross and the Prodigal*, 55–56, 69–70.

The meeting of the younger son and his father shows us that our Father's mercy is an undeserved gift of his goodness. Like the younger son in the parable, we do not deserve any special treatment from our Father, and he is under no obligation to forgive us and take us back. When we repent, we throw ourselves completely upon the Father's mercy and goodness. Like the father in the parable, our heavenly Father is "filled with compassion" (Luke 15:20).[21] His goodness and mercy are so great that he will always take us back when we repent and return to him, no matter how great and how many are our sins.

By giving us the forgiveness petition, Jesus summons us not only to repent of our sins but also to have trust and confidence in the Father's merciful love. For our Father is "merciful and gracious, slow to anger, and abounding in steadfast love" (Exod. 34:6), and "he delights in showing clemency" (Mic. 7:18). Our Father is watching and waiting for us to come home to him. He cannot wait to run out and greet us with open arms to welcome us back to himself.

Second, when we pray the forgiveness petition, we commit ourselves to imitate the Father's ways of goodness and forgiveness in our dealings with others, for we ask the Father to forgive us in light of our forgiving those who wrong us. As we discussed in chapter 2, the Father wants to form his people so that our lives will reflect his own goodness and compassion. Part of Jesus's revelatory teaching, therefore, involves instructing us how to live in a manner pleasing to the Father. For instance, in Luke 6, Jesus concludes his teaching on genuine love as selflessly doing good for others with the exhortation "Be merciful, just as your Father is merciful" (v. 36). As the Father is loving, compassionate, and forgiving, so should Jesus's disciples be loving, compassionate, and forgiving. For then, Jesus says, "You will be children of the Most High" (6:35). When his children learn

---

21. The Greek word in Luke 15:20 for "filled with compassion" (*splanchnizomai*) appears elsewhere in Luke. It names the deep feeling that Jesus has for the widow of Nain who is in the funeral procession for her only son (7:13) and that the good Samaritan has for the wounded, left-for-dead Jewish traveler (10:33). It is, as the Canticle of Zechariah puts it, the "tender mercy" and compassion that God has for his people "who sit in darkness and in the shadow of death" (1:77–78).

from and imitate the Father's ways, the Father's own compassion and forgiveness radiate out through their lives.

Jesus's instruction for us to imitate our Father's compassion and forgiveness in our dealings with others gives us perspective on the subordinate clause of the forgiveness petition. In Matthew, we ask the Father to forgive us in a manner comparable to how we forgive others: "*as* we also have forgiven our debtors" (6:12, emphasis added). In Luke, the relation is more causal: we ask for mercy "*for* we ourselves forgive everyone" (11:4, emphasis added). Either way, in the forgiveness petition, we are asking the Father to forgive us in the same way that we forgive others who wrong us.

Such a connection between God's forgiving us and our forgiving others appears in Jewish tradition as well as in several of Jesus's sayings. In Sirach, we read, "Forgive your neighbor the wrong he has done, and then your sins will be pardoned when you pray" (28:2). Sirach later adds, "If one has no mercy toward another like himself, can he then seek pardon for his own sins" (28:4)?

Matthew's Gospel brings out strongly this connection between the Father's forgiving us and our forgiving of others. Included among the Beatitudes is the declaration "Blessed are the merciful, for they will receive mercy" (Matt. 5:7). Jesus emphasizes this connection in the words that immediately follow the Lord's Prayer: "For if you forgive others their trespasses, your heavenly Father will also forgive you; but if you do not forgive others, neither will your Father forgive your trespasses" (6:14–15). For his part, Luke includes this claim in his Sermon on the Plain: "Forgive, and you will be forgiven" (6:37). Both of these sayings resonate with Jesus's words in Mark 11:25: "Whenever you stand praying, forgive, if you have anything against anyone; so that your Father in heaven may also forgive you your trespasses."

Much as the parable of the prodigal son provides us with dramatic insights into sin, repentance, and the Father's mercy, so can we gain insight into the connection between the Father's forgiving us and our forgiving others by examining the parable of the unforgiving servant (Matt. 18:23–35). The parable of the unforgiving servant appears in the so-called life in the church discourse (18:1–35), the fourth of the five major teaching discourses that Jesus delivers in Matthew. Jesus addresses this discourse to his disciples, instructing them on how they are to live as members of his church. Among the topics in this discourse are the importance of humility (18:1–5), the gravity of sin, the need to root out its causes (18:6–9), the ways to deal with members who stray and may even refuse to repent (18:10–20), and, significant for our purposes, the need of Jesus's disciples to be forgiving without measure.

The parable is introduced by Peter's question about how often he must forgive a brother who repeatedly sins against him and whether a limit should be set at seven times (Matt. 18:21). Jesus responds by saying that no limit should be set on how often we must forgive those who wrong us: "Not seven times, but, I tell you, seventy-seven times" (18:22). The mention of "seventy-seven" here recalls the figure of Lamech in Genesis 4:24. Appearing in the genealogy of Cain, Lamech undertakes a campaign of disproportionate revenge against someone who wronged him: "If Cain is avenged sevenfold, truly Lamech seventy-sevenfold."[22] Lamech's vengeance serves as the point of contrast with what Jesus teaches about forgiveness—namely, our forgiveness must be unlimited and unmeasured with respect to the wrongs done to us.

Jesus elaborates on this need for his disciples to show unlimited forgiveness by telling the parable of the unforgiving servant. This parable uses the same economic language for sin and forgiveness as the Lord's Prayer: "debt" (*opheilē*), "debtors" (*opheiletēs*), and "forgiving" (*aphiēmi*) debts. This economic language provides the metaphorical register for responding to the questions about sin and forgiveness that prompted this parable.[23]

The parable begins with a king who decides that it is time to collect on debts that are owed to him by his servants. Brought before the

22. Gen. 4:23–24 reads, "Lamech said to his wives: . . . I have killed a man for wounding me, a young man for striking me. If Cain is avenged sevenfold, truly Lamech seventy-sevenfold."
23. See Eubank, *Wages of Cross-Bearing*, 53–63.

king is a servant who is in debt to the king for "ten thousand talents" (Matt. 18:24). In Greco-Roman antiquity, a talent was a very large unit of weight and currency.[24] Weighing in at ten thousand talents, the amount of money this servant owes the king is astronomically large, a sum that the servant could never pay back. As one might expect in the ancient world, the king orders that the servant and his family be sold into slavery and his property liquidated in order to raise money to pay off his debt. The servant, however, throws himself down before the king and begs for mercy: "[He] fell on his knees before [the king], saying, 'Have patience with me, and I will pay you everything'" (18:26). The servant's words here are something of a hopeless last resort, for his debt is so absurdly huge that he could never repay it.

And yet, the king feels "pity" for this servant, and then the king "released him and forgave him the debt" (Matt. 18:27). The term for what the king feels for this pleading servant, translated here as "pity" (*splanchnistheis*; 18:27), is the same Greek word for the "compassion" (*esplanchnisthē*) the father in the parable of the prodigal son feels when he sees the younger son off in the distance, coming back home (Luke 15:20). As the father forgave the great wrongs done to him by his younger son, so here the king forgives the very great debt owed him by this servant. The king does so out of his generous goodness and compassion.

The parable then shifts to a dispute between the servant and one of his own debtors, a peer who owes him "a hundred denarii" (Matt. 18:28). A denarius was a Roman coin, and by way of comparison, in the early Roman Empire, 225 denarii was the annual salary of a Roman soldier.[25] One hundred denarii, therefore, is a significant debt, but it is one that could reasonably be paid off in time. Moreover, it also pales in comparison to the ten thousand talents the servant owes the king. Not only is the amount of debt owed far less in this case, but the relationship between the servant and his debtor is one between social equals (and not between a king and a subordinate).

24. See Davies and Allison, *Gospel according to Saint Matthew*, 2:798.
25. A. Anderson, "Imperial Army," 93.

The debtor says and does the same thing the servant himself had said and done to the king: "[He] fell down and pleaded with him, 'Have patience with me, and I will pay you'" (Matt. 18:29; cf. 18:27). And yet, the servant does not treat his debtor in the same way the king treated him. He has his debtor imprisoned (another common way of dealing with unpaid debts in antiquity) until he or his family can come up with the money to pay off his debt.[26]

When news of this reaches the king, he again summons his servant and chastises him for not treating his own debtor in the same manner as the king treated him (Matt. 18:32–33). The king had shown great mercy to the servant, forgiving his astronomical debt and thus delivering him from a hopeless situation—and all this for a subordinate who did not deserve any such treatment. Moreover, the king's words imply that he had expected the servant to learn from his experience of being forgiven and thus show mercy to others in turn: "Should you not have had mercy on your fellow slave, as I had mercy on you?" (18:33). The king then orders this unforgiving servant to be given "over to be tortured until he would pay his entire debt" (18:34). Torture was seemingly a feature of life in debt prison,[27] and in some circles, physical punishment was reckoned as a way to pay off debts.[28] The parable ends with Jesus bringing this parable to bear on our being forgiven by the Father and the Father's desire that we in turn forgive others: "So my heavenly Father will also do to every one of you, if you do not forgive your brother or sister from your heart" (18:35).

Jesus's concluding statement in Matthew 18:35 illumines the condition expressed in the subordinate clause of the forgiveness petition that connects the Father's forgiving us, especially at the moment of judgment, with our practice of forgiving those who have wronged us throughout life. In the parable, the king (i.e., the Father) is compas-

26. Eubank, *Wages of Cross-Bearing*, 59; Eubank, "Prison, Penance or Purgatory," 163–67.
27. Eubank, "Prison, Penance or Purgatory," 164–65.
28. G. Anderson, *Sin*, 8–9, 29–30, 32–33.

sionate and very generous in forgiving sins. He remits his servant's absurdly large debt out of his great compassion, and in doing so, the king delivers the servant from a hopeless situation. As we are invited to see ourselves in the figure of the servant, Jesus teaches us that we owe a debt to God because of our sins—and we really cannot even imagine the magnitude of this sin debt. Moreover, like the servant's situation in the parable, ours is a debt beyond our capacity to pay off. It is the perfectly righteous act of love and obedience of Jesus, giving his life on the cross, that pays off the debt of sins and thus obtains pardon from the Father.[29]

Having shown us such great compassion and forgiveness, the Father wants us to be similarly compassionate toward and forgiving of those who wrong us—as the subordinate clause of the forgiveness petition implies. As with the servant and his debtor, the wrongs that others cause us are real and significant. But they are also far smaller in scale than the debt we incur with the Father through our sins. In the parable, the king expected the servant to learn from his experience of being forgiven and imitate the king's ways by showing similar forgiveness to others.[30] The servant, however, did not forgive but instead resorted to an established means for exacting repayment of a debt in antiquity (i.e., he had his debtor imprisoned). Upon learning of the servant's conduct, the king then dealt with the servant in a comparable manner to how the servant had dealt with his own debtor. The parable thus displays what the condition in the subordinate clause indicates: at the moment of judgment, the Father will treat us in a manner comparable to how we forgive or refuse to forgive those who have wronged us during our lives.

Nathan Eubank has called attention to another teaching in the Sermon on the Mount that illumines both the forgiveness petition and the parable of the unforgiving servant: "The measure you give will be the measure you get" (Matt. 7:2). Building on the work of

29. See Eubank, *Wages of Cross-Bearing*, chaps. 4–5.
30. Cf. Sir. 28:4: "If one has no mercy toward another like himself, can he then seek pardon for his own sins?"

Bernard Couroyer, Eubank shows that this saying reflects practices associated with business transactions and the repayment of loans in kind; the same container would be used for both the taking out and the repayment of a loan.[31] The upshot of Jesus's teaching in Matthew 7:2, Eubank writes, is that "God will judge a person using the same standard of judgment that that person used in judging others."[32] This is the sense of the relationship between the Father's forgiving us at the moment of judgment and our forgiving others throughout our lives: "Forgive us our debts, as we also have forgiven our debtors" (11:12).

It is part of our fallen human nature that we can often find it difficult to forgive others who wrong us—and even forgive ourselves for the bad things we do. Forgiveness is not easy. It does not mean ignoring the wrong, denying that something bad has happened, or overlooking the real wounds that have been caused. Rather, forgiveness means to choose love and compassion despite the hurt and the injustice.[33] It is to choose love over vengeance, compassion over hatred, reconciliation over resentment. It is, as Paul writes, to "overcome evil with good" (Rom. 12:21).

Forgiveness also brings freedom and healing. When we forgive those who wrong us—or at least commit to work toward forgiving them—the power of those wounds inflicted on us begins to wane. Put conversely, clinging to past hurts, holding grudges, and nurturing resentments over wrongs done can exacerbate a bad situation by making us prisoners of our own pain and misery. The older son in the parable of the prodigal son displays something of this. His hurt and resentment keep him from entering the feast. His self-righteousness and indignation keep him from recognizing his father's goodness as well as his own need to repent and imitate his father's ways. The

31. Eubank, *Wages of Cross-Bearing*, 64–67. He writes (*Wages of Cross-Bearing*, 66), "The best way to ensure that someone pays exactly what is owed is to require him to repay his debt with the same measure that he used to measure out the loan in the first place."

32. Eubank, *Wages of Cross-Bearing*, 65.

33. I owe this expression to Michelle Wright.

parable ends without telling us how the older son responds to the father's invitation, although we as readers know what he ought to do.

In his explication of the Sermon on the Mount, Augustine comments that forgiveness is what Jesus prescribes as a remedy for such misery. He sees a special place for the forgiveness petition in the Lord's Prayer because Jesus repeats the conditional connection between the Father's forgiving us and our forgiving others immediately after teaching the Lord's Prayer (Matt. 6:14–15). Augustine writes, "Of all the pronouncements in which the Lord has ordered us to pray, He has deliberately attached a very special commendation to the pronouncement which deals with the forgiving of sins. In this pronouncement He wished us to be merciful because that is the only prescribed means of avoiding miseries."[34] By repeating this condition, Jesus teaches us the indispensable need for his disciples to be forgiving of others. For forgiveness, as Augustine puts it, "is the only prescribed means of avoiding miseries."

Conclusion

The forgiveness petition is a prayer of repentance. We acknowledge that we are sinners who have offended the Father, and we ask the Father to forgive us for what we have done. As displayed in the two parables discussed here, the Father is unimaginably good, compassionate, and forgiving. There are no sins too great, no debts too large, that the Father will not readily forgive those who ask him. The Father's ways are love, compassion, and forgiveness, and he seeks to form us to be similarly loving, compassionate, and forgiving. As a way to facilitate our imitation of the Father's ways, we ask the Father to forgive us in light of our forgiving those who have wronged us. Forgiving others is not easy, and indeed, we should ask the Lord to help us to forgive those who hurt us. But neither is forgiveness optional for Jesus's disciples, nor is it a peripheral element of the

---

34. Augustine, *Commentary on the Lord's Sermon on the Mount* 2.11.39 (Kavanagh, 148).

Christian life. Rather, it is a central and necessary part of life for those who wish to follow Jesus. This is because love, compassion, and forgiveness are the ways of the Father. To those who learn from the Father and are "merciful, just as your Father is merciful" (Luke 6:36), Jesus says, "Your reward will be great, and you will be children of the Most High" (6:35).

7

Deliver Us

In the closing petitions of the Lord's Prayer, we ask the Father to help us in our struggle against the lure of sin and the powers of evil. Both Matthew and Luke give the same wording for the third "we" petition, wherein we pray to the Father, "Do not bring us to the time of trial" (Matt. 6:13 // Luke 11:4). Matthew's version has another petition that resembles the previous one in both theme and substance: "But rescue us from the evil one" (6:13). By giving us these petitions, Jesus teaches us that life in the world is a spiritual battle. As we read in Ephesians 6:12, "Our struggle is not against enemies of blood and flesh, but against the rulers, against the authorities, against the cosmic powers of this present darkness, against the spiritual forces of evil."[1]

The arrangement of the final "we" petitions resembles the arrangement of the final "you" petitions. The last of the shared "you" petitions is the kingdom petition—"Your kingdom come"—and both Matthew and Luke give the same wording for it (Matt. 6:10 // Luke 11:2). Similarly, the last of the shared "we" petitions is "And do not bring us to the time of trial" (Matt. 6:13 // Luke 11:4)—and here too, Matthew and Luke provide the same wording. After the last of the shared "you" and "we" petitions, Matthew has another

1. See Schlier, *Principalities and Powers.*

petition that expands on the preceding one. In the "you" petitions, Matthew has the will petition, which develops the substance of the kingdom petition: when the Father brings his heavenly kingdom to earth, then his will is going to be done on earth as it is in heaven. Similarly, Matthew follows up the petition "Do not bring us to the time of trial" with the request "Rescue us from the evil one" (6:13). Seen in this light, the petition for "rescue" (or deliverance) "from the evil one" elaborates on the substance of the petition about "the time of trial." Given the close connections between these petitions, we will take them together and refer to them as two parts of a petition for deliverance.

The language of these petitions poses some unique challenges for understanding their theological substance. For instance, the NRSV translates the first part of the petition as "Do not bring us to the time of trial" (Matt. 6:13 // Luke 11:4). Arguably, most English-speaking Christians know this petition in the translation given in the KJV and others: "Lead us not into temptation." How are we to understand the Greek word *peirasmos*, translated respectively as "the time of trial" or "temptation"? Similarly, in the second part of the deliverance petition, the NRSV reads, "Rescue us from the evil one" (Matt. 6:13). Here too, most English-speaking Christians know a different translation: "Deliver us from evil." Is the petition asking for deliverance from Satan specifically or evil in a more general, abstract sense? Moreover, there is the theologically challenging matter that the language of the first part of the petition suggests: In what sense could the Father bring or not bring "us to the time of trial" (Matt. 6:13)? Accordingly, the language of the deliverance petition requires more extensive exploration than that in other petitions.

Approaching these issues with the awareness that the plain sense can support a variety of meanings, we will argue that when we pray the deliverance petition, *we ask the Father to keep us faithful to him when the devil presses his attack on us, especially in moments of intense, ultimate crisis.*

▨ The Language of the Deliverance Petition

"Do Not Bring Us to the Time of Trial"

The NRSV translates the first part of the deliverance petition as "Do not bring us to the time of trial" (Matt. 6:13 // Luke 11:4).[2] The expression "do not bring" (*mē eisenenkēs*) is a verbal construction for "'absolute' prohibitions that forbid the performance of an action as a whole."[3] Moreover, this verb has as its subject the second-person singular "you." In the context of the Lord's Prayer, this "you" refers to the Father. The petition points to the Father as the one who can "bring us to the time of trial" and also refrain from doing so (Matt. 6:13 // Luke 11:4). These grammatical considerations show this first part of the petition to be an ardent plea: we are begging that the Father "not bring us to the time of trial."

The Greek word translated in the NRSV as "time of trial" is *peirasmos*. This noun is related to the Greek verb *peirazō*, which can mean "to tempt" or "to test."[4] In the Old Testament, we find instances where God tests people's faith and obedience. Arguably, the most famous biblical example of such testing is Abraham's binding of Isaac (Gen. 22:1–19).[5] Conversely, we also see infamous cases where people put God to the test or called on God to prove himself by performing some request (e.g., Exod. 17:2, 7; Isa. 7:12). A famous scriptural case of this is when the Israelites call on the Lord to produce water for them in the wilderness and so prove himself to them (Exod. 17:7).

Theologically speaking, God's testing people's faith and obedience is something altogether different from temptation in the customary

---

2. Matthew and Luke provide the same wording for this petition: *kai mē eisenenkēs hēmas eis peirasmon*.

3. Béchard, *Syntax of New Testament Greek*, §3.2 (p. 39). The construction is that of an aorist subjunctive verb (*eisenenkēs*) with the negative particle *mē*.

4. In the LXX, *peirazō* almost always renders the Hebrew verb *nissâ* (save Ps. 34:16; Dan. 12:10). For examples of *peirazō* as "to test" in the LXX, see Gen. 22:1; Exod. 16:4; 17:2, 7; Ps. 94:9. For examples in the New Testament, see Mark 8:11; 10:2; 1 Cor. 10:9; Heb. 3:9.

5. Gen. 22:1 makes clear that the binding of Isaac is a test of Abraham: "After these things God tested [Hb. *nissâ*; Gk. *epeirazen*] Abraham."

sense of the term. Temptation is luring people to commit sin, and ingredient to the nature of sin is its being contrary to God's goodness and will. God, who is goodness itself, does not do this. As James teaches us quite plainly, "No one, when tempted, should say, 'I am being tempted by God'; for God cannot be tempted by evil and he himself tempts no one" (James 1:13). So when we petition the Father "Do not bring us to the time of trial" (Matt. 6:13 // Luke 11:4), it should not be taken to imply that the Father would actively tempt us to sin.[6]

To understand what the petition envisions by the Father's action here, many have called attention to an evening prayer recorded in the Babylonian Talmud.[7] The pertinent section of the prayer reads, "And bring me not into sin, or into iniquity, or into temptation, or into contempt. And may the good inclination have sway over me and let not the evil inclination have sway over me."[8] Joachim Jeremias argues that the verbal syntax in this part of the prayer does not envision "an unmediated action of God but his permission which allows something to happen."[9] That is, the expression "bring me not into sin" is a request for God's help to remain faithful in times of temptation.

Understood in this light, this part of the deliverance petition does not imply that the Father would tempt us to sin. Rather, it is a petition whereby we ask the Father to help us to remain faithful and obedient to him when we are tempted. As Jeremias writes, the petition "does not request that he who prays may be spared temptation, but that God may help him to overcome it."[10]

6. In 2017, Pope Francis voiced support for modifying the conventional Italian translation of this petition (*non ci indurre in tentazione*) in the version of the Lord's Prayer that is recited in Italian liturgy. This change was later made so as to avoid giving the (mistaken) impression that God actively tempts someone to sin—and the former Italian phrasing lends itself to more such a misunderstanding than the usual English rendering does. For perspective on this matter (including the specific Italian language issues involved), see Roza, "Pope Francis and the Our Father."

7. Strack and Billerbeck, *Das Evangelium*, 1:422; Jeremias, *Prayers of Jesus*, 105.

8. b. Ber. 60b (Epstein and Simon, 378).

9. Jeremias, *Prayers of Jesus*, 105. He argues that the verbal constructions in this prayer are "causative forms . . . [with] a permissive nuance" (105).

10. Jeremias, *Prayers of Jesus*, 105.

There is also the matter of what is meant by "the time of trial" or "temptation." As mentioned above, the Greek term here is *peirasmos*, and in the New Testament, this noun has a variety of similar (and sometimes overlapping) meanings.[11] In some places, the word means "temptation" in the usual sense of enticement to commit sin, such as when the devil tempts Jesus in the wilderness after his baptism.[12] In other places, this word can mean a "hardship" or a "testing."[13] At the Last Supper, Jesus says to the twelve apostles, "You are those who have stood by me in my trials [*peirasmois*]" (Luke 22:28). Relatedly, the verb *peirazō* can describe the actions of opponents who test Jesus with their questions.[14]

A third sense of the noun *peirasmos* may be its least familiar meaning, but it is arguably the sense in the forefront of the deliverance petition. Some Jewish scenarios of the end-time, given in both the Scriptures and Jewish writings outside of the canon, envision an especially intense period of suffering for God's people (and sometimes their foes as well) that immediately precedes God's end-time action and the subsequent arrival of the eschatological age.[15] For instance, Daniel 12:1 says of this time, "There shall be a time of anguish, such as has never occurred since nations first came into existence." Some writings use the image of a woman in labor to signify this time of eschatological suffering wherein a period of intense pain gives way to joy and the arrival of a new life (Isa. 26:16–19; John 16:21; Rev. 12:1–6). Examples from Jewish writings outside of the Scripture likewise attest to forms of such eschatological expectation.[16]

11. See "πειρασμός," in BAGD, 640–41.
12. Matt. 4:1, 3; Luke 4:2; cf. 1 Cor. 10:13; 1 Tim. 6:9.
13. Luke 8:13; Acts. 20:19; Gal. 4:14; Heb. 3:8; James 1:2, 12; 1 Pet. 1:6; 4:12; perhaps 2 Pet. 2:9.
14. Matt. 16:1; 19:3; 22:18, 35; Luke 11:16. Recalling the LXX usage, the same language is used in the New Testament to talk about tempting God (e.g., Acts 5:9; 15:10; 1 Cor. 10:9; Heb. 3:9; James 1:13).
15. See Allison, *End of the Ages*, 5–25; Aune, *Revelation 1–5*, 239–40; Pitre, *Jesus, the Tribulation*, esp. 41–130; Watson, "Tribulation," 1335.
16. Allison (*End of the Ages*, 5–25) mentions a number of examples, including 1 En. 99–100; 4 Ezra 5:1–13; 6:21–23; 2 Bar. 25–29.

This period of intense suffering that immediately precedes God's end-time action and his establishing the eschatological state of affairs goes by different names, such as the messianic woes, the tribulation, or the affliction.[17] Revelation 3:10 refers to this time of intense, eschatological suffering with the same word as in the Lord's Prayer: *peirasmos*. The text reads, "Because you have kept my word of patient endurance, I will keep you from the hour of trial [*tou peirasmou*] that is coming on the whole world to test [*peirasai*] the inhabitants of the earth."

While the matter is debated, I agree with those who take the mention of *peirasmos* or "time of trial" in the Lord's Prayer to refer primarily to this intense, eschatological situation of suffering.[18] This interpretation finds support from a number of connections between the Lord's Prayer and the accounts of Jesus in Gethsemane, where the term *peirasmos* also occurs in the sense of the eschatological trial. In Matthew, the account of Jesus in Gethsemane is the only place where the term *peirasmos* occurs besides the Lord's Prayer, and Luke similarly uses the term here.[19] Not only does this term appear both in the Lord's Prayer and in the Gethsemane accounts, but it is also used in both places in connection with prayer, verbs of motion, and the Greek preposition *eis* ("into"). In the Lord's Prayer, we pray to the Father not to "bring" us "into the time of trial" (*eis peirasmon*; Matt. 6:13 alt.; Luke 11:4). In Gethsemane, Jesus similarly exhorts his apostles to "pray," specifically that they "may not come into the time of trial [*eis peirasmon*]" (Matt. 26:41 // Luke 22:46). To reiterate what was discussed previously, there are other connections between the Lord's Prayer and the Gethsemane accounts. Recoiling at the

17. The Hebrew and Greek versions of Dan. 12:1 refer to this time with the following terms: Hb. *ṣārâ*; Gk. *thlipsis*.

18. So too Brown, "Pater Noster," 248–51; Davies and Allison, *Gospel according to Saint Matthew*, 1:613–14; Jeremias, *Prayers of Jesus*, 105–6.

19. In Matthew, the only uses of the noun *peirasmos* are in the Lord's Prayer (6:13) and in Gethsemane (26:41). In addition to these two parallel locations (Luke 11:4; 22:40, 46), Luke's Gospel features the term in 4:13 (after Jesus's temptations in the wilderness), 8:13 (the interpretation of the parable of the sower), and 22:28 (the Last Supper saying cited above).

prospect of his impending suffering and death, Jesus himself prays and uses the same address that he instructed his disciples to use in their prayer: "Father" (Matt. 26:39 // Luke 22:42).[20] Jesus instructs his disciples to pray to the Father, "Your will be done" (Matt. 6:10), and in Gethsemane, Jesus himself prays to the Father with the exact same words: "Your will be done" (Matt. 26:42).[21]

These similarities between the Lord's Prayer and Gethsemane invite us to see these two parts of the Gospel in relation. The term *peirasmos* has an eschatological meaning in the Gethsemane episode, and we can understand it the same way in the Lord's Prayer. But the language of the Lord's Prayer can also be taken as speaking secondarily to temptation in the general sense of the word. And so, to maintain both the connection and the distinction between these two senses of *peirasmos*, we will refer to them respectively as "temptation" (i.e., enticement to sin) and "eschatological temptation" or "trial" (i.e., an intense, ultimate time of affliction).

The Gospels also associate *peirasmos*—in the sense of both temptation to sin and eschatological trial—with the demonic. Recognition of this demonic association gives us insight into both the first part of the petition ("Do not bring us to the time of trial") and the second part of the deliverance petition, which appears only in Matthew: "Rescue us from the evil one" (6:13).[22]

"Rescue Us from the Evil One"

The verb in the second part of the deliverance petition, translated as "rescue," is *rhyomai*. Like most other verbs in the Lord's Prayer, the verb "rescue" (*rhysai*) is an aorist imperative. In the Greek edition of the Old Testament (the LXX), this verb often designates the actions of God to rescue his people from danger or bad situations, such as

20. Note Jesus's first-person singular use of "my Father" in Matt. 26:39 in comparison to the general address "our Father."
21. The Greek wording of Matt. 6:10 and 26:42 is identical: *genēthētō to thelēma sou*.
22. The Greek text of Matt. 6:13b reads as follows: *rhysai hēmas apo tou ponērou*.

at the sea crossing in the exodus (Exod. 14:30 LXX) and at the future eschatological restoration of Israel (Isa. 52:9 LXX).

The NRSV specifies the danger from which we ask the Father to rescue us as "the evil one" (*tou ponērou*; Matt. 6:13). Here too, most English-speaking Christians know the translation of this petition as "Deliver us from evil." Ancient Greek is a gendered language, and the Greek word *ponērou* could be either masculine (i.e., "evil one") or neuter (i.e., "evil"). While both readings are grammatically possible, it is more likely that Matthew invites us to see this petition as referring primarily to the devil.[23]

There are several indicators in Matthew's Gospel that support this conclusion. First, grammatically, the phrase "from the evil one" (*apo tou ponērou*) employs the definite article "the" (*tou*; Matt. 6:13). The phrase most easily reads as "the evil one." Second, Matthew uses the same phrase elsewhere in his Gospel to designate the devil. When Jesus interprets the parable of the sower, the birds who eat the seed on the path symbolize the action of "the evil one" (*ho ponēros*) who "snatches away what is sown in the heart" (13:19). Jesus also uses this language to interpret the parable of the weeds and the wheat: "The weeds are the children of the evil one [*tou ponērou*], and the

23. Christian orthodoxy (which this book embraces) understands the devil to be a real, spiritual being and not a symbol, metaphor, or mythological personification of evil. As the Nicene Creed declares, God the Father is the Creator of "all things visible and invisible." The invisible things created by God are the angels. These are creatures of pure spirit, and like all things made by God, all angels are created good (cf. Gen. 1). Angels also have intellects and free wills, and thus they have the capacity to love, honor, and obey God—or to refuse to do so. Those angels who refuse to love, honor, and obey God (and their choice is permanent because of their higher mode of existence) become irrevocably corrupted by their actions and are thus known as demons. Biblical revelation teaches that the most powerful of the angels who so rebelled against God and led other angels into rebellion is known as Lucifer or Satan. The everlasting defeat of Satan and the ransoming of sinners from his claim are secured by the death and resurrection of Jesus. Until Christ's parousia, the devil and those demonic spirits in league with him "make war on . . . those who keep the commandments of God and hold the testimony of Jesus" (Rev. 12:17). They strive to get people to refuse God and rebel against him by sinning and so come to share their own miserable fate in hell. For a helpful study of the theology of angels and their activities, see Bonino, *Angels and Demons*.

enemy who sowed them is the devil" (13:38–39). At the harvest (i.e., the end-time judgment), these weeds are separated and thrown into the fire (13:42), the same fate that is elsewhere said to be "prepared for the devil and his angels" (25:41). Third, as we will see, Matthew's Gospel associates with the devil both tempting and the eschatological trial. Accordingly, it is preferable to take the deliverance petition as asking the Father specifically to rescue us from the power of Satan.

Both parts of the deliverance petition are similar in theme and substance. The "time of trial" (*peirasmos*) to which we ask the Father not to bring us does not primarily concern temptation to sin in the ordinary sense (although the language can accommodate that interpretation secondarily). Rather, we ask the Father to preserve us in a situation of intense, eschatological trial, wherein Satan and the powers of darkness throw all that they can at us in order to get us to reject God. The deliverance petition, "Rescue us from the evil one," thus elaborates on the substance of "Do not bring us to the time of trial." Hence, we ask the Father to deliver us from the devil's assaults, especially in moments of intense, ultimate crisis.

Exposition of the Deliverance Petition

We can gain insight into the deliverance petition by examining the Gospel accounts wherein Jesus himself undergoes both temptation and eschatological trial as well as his teachings about his disciples' experiences of these situations. We will see that what is the case for Jesus in these matters will analogously be the case for his disciples.

Jesus, Temptations, the Eschatological Trial, and the Evil One

Matthew and Luke present Jesus as undergoing both temptations to sin and the eschatological trial. We see the first in the accounts of Jesus's temptations in the wilderness (Matt. 4:1–11 // Luke 4:1–13). Throughout these accounts, Matthew and Luke identify the devil as the one who does the tempting (Matt. 4:1, 3; Luke 4:1–2), and both evangelists use the language of *peirasmos* (either in noun or in verb form) to characterize the devil's activity (Matt. 4:1, 3; Luke 4:2, 13).[24] These are temptations in the proper sense because the devil is enticing Jesus to sin by acting as the Son of God and messiah in a manner contrary to the Father's will.[25] He tempts Jesus to use his power to satisfy bodily desires by turning stones into food after a long fast (Matt. 4:2–4; Luke 4:2–4). The devil then tempts Jesus by asking him to jump off the top of the Jerusalem temple, the most important structure in the most important biblical city. By doing so, he would attempt to force the Father's hand to save him and thus make a grand public display of his identity as the Son (Matt. 4:5–7; Luke 4:9–12). Satan then tempts Jesus with the world's wealth and power, which he offers in exchange for worship (Matt. 4:8–10; Luke 4:5–8). At a basic level, these are all perennial temptations to acquire bodily pleasure, fame, wealth, and power by committing sin.[26]

Satan begins two of the three temptations with the phrase "If you are the Son of God . . ." (Matt. 4:3, 6; Luke 4:3, 9). Given that in the biblical tradition an ideal son learns from and obeys his father, Jesus shows himself to be the Father's obedient and faithful Son precisely by not giving in to the devil's temptations.[27] The temptation narratives also show Jesus embodying perfectly Israel's vocation as God's "firstborn son" (Exod. 4:22). Whereas the Israelites tested the Lord in the wilderness (Exod. 17:1–7), grumbled and rebelled against him (Exod. 16:7–9; 17:3; Num. 14:27, 29; 16:11), and sinned (Exod. 32:1–6; Num. 25:1–9), Jesus remains faithful and obedient when he is similarly tempted in the wilderness and refuses to test his Father.

24. Matt. 4:3 identifies the devil as "the tempter" (*ho peirazōn*).
25. Francis Martin writes, Jesus "was tempted by Satan to be a Messiah other than the one willed by the Father, to be a Messiah who would perform spectacular works that would force a superficial allegiance" (*Fire in the Cloud*, 34).
26. They resemble what 1 John 2:16 lists as what abides in the fallen world: "the desire of the flesh, the desire of the eyes, and the pride of life" (my translation).
27. As Heb. 4:15 teaches, Jesus "in every respect has been tested [*pepeirasmenon*] as we are, yet without sin."

In addition to these temptations to sin, Jesus undergoes the intense, eschatological trial in the events of his passion.[28] In Gethsemane, Jesus is "deeply grieved, even to death" (Matt. 26:38), and in Luke's account, he experiences "anguish" (*agōnia*; Luke 22:44). As mentioned above, in both Matthew and Luke, Jesus tells his apostles, "Pray that you may not come into the time of trial [*eis peirasmon*]" (Matt. 26:41; Luke 22:40; 22:46; cf. Mark 14:38). This injunction that the disciples pray "not [to] come into the time of trial" seems to imply that Jesus himself *is* entering into this eschatological trial in his passion.[29]

In Gethsemane, Jesus faces the ultimate choice of his life: Will he embrace the cross in obedience to his Father's will for him—that is, drink "the cup" (Matt. 26:39; cf. Luke 22:42)?[30] Despite his natural recoiling at the prospect of suffering, shame, and a horrible death, Jesus agrees to do the Father's will in words that recall (and quote) the Lord's Prayer: "If this cannot pass unless I drink it, your will be done" (Matt. 26:42; cf. Luke 22:42). Once again, Jesus shows himself to be the Father's faithful Son by committing himself fully to obeying the Father's will (Matt. 26:39; Luke 22:42).

That Jesus undergoes eschatological testing in the events of his passion is underscored by the activity of Satan in these events.[31] Luke concludes his account of Jesus's temptations in the wilderness by remarking that the devil "departed from him until an opportune time" (4:13). This "opportune time" comes in the events of Jesus's passion. When Luke begins his passion narrative, he specifies that Satan had taken possession of Judas and so orchestrated the betrayal of Jesus by one of his closest associates (22:3; cf. John 13:2, 27). After Judas betrays Jesus in Gethsemane, Jesus announces to the arrest party that this is "the power of darkness" (Luke 22:53).

28. Forms of this claim have been advanced by many, including Albert Schweitzer in his *Quest for the Historical Jesus*, 387–91.
29. See Brown, *Death of the Messiah*, 1:158–62.
30. On the image of "the cup," see Luz, *Matthew 8–20*, 543, and references in 543n17; Luz, *Matthew 21–28*, 396.
31. See Brown, "Pater Noster," 250–51.

Matthew likewise points to the action of Satan in the eschatological testing that is Jesus's passion, albeit in a subtle way. As mentioned above, when tempting Jesus in the wilderness, the devil introduces two of the temptations with the phrase "If you are the Son of God . . ." (Matt. 4:3, 6). This same language reappears at Jesus's crucifixion, where the passersby taunt the crucified Jesus: "If you are the Son of God, come down from the cross" (27:40). In the words of the passersby, we hear echoes of Satan's voice, tempting Jesus to disobey the Father and come off the cross to save his mortal life. But as in the wilderness, Jesus again shows himself to be the Son of God by remaining perfectly faithful and obedient to the Father, even unto death.

This review of Gospel episodes wherein Jesus undergoes both temptations to sin and the intense eschatological trial illumines both parts of the deliverance petition. First, the devil is at work in both temptations to sin and the eschatological trial. He tempts Jesus to sin in the wilderness, and when Jesus enters the eschatological trial in his passion, the devil brings all that he can, "the power of darkness" (Luke 22:53), against Jesus. Seen in this light, the petition "Do not bring us to the time of trial" implies what Matthew's version of the Lord's Prayer makes explicit with "Rescue us from the evil one" (Matt. 6:13). Second, in both the temptations to sin and the eschatological trial, the devil works to get Jesus to disobey the Father's will. Whether in the wilderness, in Gethsemane, or at the cross, the devil tempts Jesus with something that is genuinely or apparently good that Jesus could have if only he would disobey the Father's will. For his part, Jesus refuses the devil's offers and instead chooses the greater good that is the Father's will. By choosing to love and obey the Father above all, Jesus reveals himself to be the Son, and he provides the example of how his disciples must live as the Father's adopted children.

Jesus's Disciples, Temptations, the Eschatological Trial, and the Evil One

Jesus's disciples must follow in the footsteps of their teacher and Lord. Just as Jesus went to the cross and so entered into the heavenly glory of the resurrection, so too must his disciples "take up their cross" (Matt. 16:24 // Luke 9:23), and they are promised heavenly rewards and life for doing so (Matt. 16:25–27 // Luke 9:24–26). A similar situation obtains with regard to both temptations to sin and the eschatological trial. As Jesus was tempted to sin by the devil, so also do the New Testament writings speak of people being similarly tempted by the devil. As Jesus entered into the eschatological trial in his passion, so also does he predict that his disciples may have to undergo this trial in some form.

While the deliverance petition primarily envisions the eschatological "time of trial," its language can accommodate temptations to sin in the ordinary sense of the word. Paul, for instance, teaches that temptations to sin are part of everyone's life experience (1 Cor. 10:13). Some of the temptations people experience come by way of the devil's instigation. In 1 Thessalonians 3, Paul reports that he sent Timothy to Thessalonica to see whether the young Christian church there had given up their faith as a result of their being harassed: "I sent to find out about your faith; I was afraid that somehow the tempter [*ho peirazōn*] had tempted [*epeirasen*] you and that our labor had been in vain" (v. 5). In 1 Corinthians 7, he instructs married couples to resume sexual relations after a mutually agreed-upon period of temporary abstinence, and this is "so that Satan may not tempt you because of your lack of self-control" (v. 5).

In one sense, when we pray, "Do not bring us to the time of trial" (Matt. 6:13 // Luke 11:4), we are asking the Father to help us to remain faithful in such moments of temptation. As Jeremias puts it, "The final petition of the Lord's Prayer [speaks] . . . not to preservation *from* temptation but to preservation *in* temptation."[32] This manner of construing the deliverance petition resonates with Paul's words in 1 Corinthians 10. Here, Paul teaches that in moments of temptation, God also provides the means to resist: "God is faithful, and he will not let you be tested beyond your strength, but with the testing he will also provide the way out so that you may be able to endure it" (v. 13).

---

32. Jeremias, *Prayers of Jesus*, 105.

However, the primary sense of "time of trial" in the Lord's Prayer is the eschatological trial. As Jesus told the apostles in Gethsemane, "Pray that you may not come into the time of trial" (Luke 22:46), so too does he instruct us to petition the Father, "Do not bring us to the time of trial" (Matt. 6:13 // Luke 11:4). Jesus undergoes the eschatological trial in the events of his passion. But what might constitute this eschatological temptation or trial for Jesus's disciples?

Jesus's apocalyptic discourse in the Synoptics sheds light on this matter (Matt. 24:1–51 // Mark 13:1–37 // Luke 21:5–36). This complex and challenging unit of material presents Jesus interconnecting the end of the Jerusalem temple with the end of the cosmic age.[33] The former is a partial and anticipatory instantiation of the latter; that is, the eschatological reality of the end of the world is partially realized in history in the destruction of the Jerusalem temple. Just as the eschatological reality of the end can be partially instantiated in historical events (before its full realization at the actual end of days), so too can the eschatological trial be partially, but genuinely, realized in the lives of his disciples throughout history. Jesus speaks in this discourse to disciples who will experience in various ways real instances of ultimate, eschatological testing.

Focusing on Matthew's version of the discourse, we find in it many conventional terms and images associated with the messianic woes or the eschatological trial. The image of a woman in labor often symbolizes the eschatological tribulation, and in the discourse, Jesus says that wars, natural disasters, and strife are only "the beginning of the birth pangs" (Matt. 24:8). In Daniel 12:1 LXX, the Greek word *thlipsis* designates this time of eschatological suffering. Similarly, in the apocalyptic discourse, Jesus states, "For at that time there will be great suffering [*thlipsis*], such as has not been from the beginning of the world until now, no, and never will be" (Matt. 24:21). Furthermore, Jesus says that in this time, "because of the increase of lawlessness [*anomian*], the love of many will grow cold" (24:12). The

---

33. For an illuminating and accessible analysis of Mark 13 along these lines, see Huizenga, *Loosing the Lion*, 270–80.

term for "lawlessness" (*anomia*) here is often used in the New Testament and other ancient Jewish texts with an eschatological sense and with demonic connotations.[34] The term, Ignace de la Potterie writes, "is essentially an eschatological term that designates the hostility and revolt of the forces of evil against the kingdom of God in the last days of the world; such hostility is characterized by its satanic aspect, by the control that is exercised by the devil."[35] Other conventional features of the eschatological trial that appear in this discourse are the presence of false messiahs and prophets (24:11, 23–26) and mass apostasy from faith. While the term *peirasmos* may not appear in Matthew 24, what the discourse describes corresponds to this same notion of the eschatological trial.

This time of demonic-influenced lawlessness will be very severe for all, including Jesus's disciples. Jesus announces that his followers will be hated, persecuted, and perhaps even killed on account of their relationship to him (Matt. 24:9). As a result of such persecutions, "Many will fall away [*skandalisthēsontai*]" (24:10). On several occasions, Matthew uses this verb, *skandalizō*, to designate those who "fall away" from their Christian faith or lead others to do so (5:29–30; 13:21; 18:6–9). So understood, the biggest temptation for Jesus's disciples in the setting of eschatological trial will be to commit apostasy—that is, to renounce God and their faith in Christ. Such a rejection of God involves the highest of stakes, for Jesus pronounces doom on those who fall away or cause others to fall away (see 5:29; 18:6–9). Conversely, Jesus encourages his disciples to remain faithful to him, even in such dire and difficult circumstances. After speaking of a wide-scale decline in love on account of this demonically inspired lawlessness, Jesus promises, "The one who endures to the end will be saved" (24:13).

In Matthew 24, Jesus speaks primarily about the eschatological trial that will be fully realized at the end of days and immediately

34. See Lyonnet and Sabourin, *Sin, Redemption, and Sacrifice*, 33–34; de la Potterie, "Sin Is Iniquity," 37–55. One thinks, for instance, of the "man of lawlessness" (2 Thess. 2:3) who appears in the eschatological scenario of 2 Thess. 2.

35. De la Potterie, "Sin Is Iniquity," 42.

precede his parousia (vv. 29–31). At the same time, the eschatological realities spoken of in this discourse were realized in a partial and anticipatory way in the destruction of the Jerusalem temple in the year 70. If we expand our interpretive focus to include other voices in the New Testament canon, we see that the eschatological trial can be realized in partial yet genuine ways in people's lives before the actual end of days. Such is the case, for instance, in the letters to the seven churches in Revelation 2–3.

The letter to the church at Smyrna (Rev. 2:8–11) addresses a poor church community that is undergoing some afflictions on account of their relations with a local synagogue that seemingly denounced them to the Roman authorities.[36] The exalted Jesus tells the Smyrnean Christians that some of them are about to be imprisoned on account of their Christian faith and that the devil is at work in this action against them. The language used to describe this imprisonment is that of the eschatological trial: "Beware, the devil is about to throw some of you into prison so that you may be tested [*peirasthēte*], and for ten days you will have affliction [*thlipsin*]. Be faithful until death, and I will give you the crown of life" (2:10). Such language suggests that this temporary affliction, which some Christians in Smyrna are about to undergo on a small scale, is a participation in the larger eschatological trial to come.

Jesus teaches that the eschatological trial he underwent in his passion is a real possibility for his followers. While it may be realized in different ways and at different moments for Jesus's disciples throughout history, the eschatological trial is an intense testing of one's fidelity and obedience to the Father and to Jesus. Much as Jesus was tempted to come off the cross and disobey the Father's will when he underwent the eschatological trial in his passion, so will Jesus's disciples be tempted to abandon their faith and turn their back on the Father in moments of intense trial. Whenever we find ourselves in situations where our fidelity to Christ and obedience to the Father lead us to encounter hatred, persecution, or suffering in some form—

---

36. On this situation, see Hemer, *Letters to the Seven Churches*, 9–12, 66–67.

and we are also enticed by the prospect of alleviating these sufferings at the cost of denying Jesus or spurning the Father's will—we are participating to some degree in the eschatological trial.

As was the case in the letter to the church at Smyrna (Rev. 2:8–11), Jesus also reveals to us that working behind the scenes in these situations of intense, ultimate crisis is the devil. He will throw all that he can at Jesus's disciples to entice or to pressure them to renounce God and their faith relationship to Jesus. Elsewhere in the Gospels, Jesus warns us strongly that the destination to which such a total (and unrepented) repudiation of God leads is hell (Matt. 5:29; 18:6–9). And it is for this very same reason that the devil so pressures and entices us to reject the Father and Christ in a definitive way. The devil wants us in hell.

Left to their own devices and abilities, Jesus's disciples cannot hope to endure such affliction and temptation. As Jesus himself declares, "If those days had not been cut short, no one would be saved; but for the sake of the elect those days will be cut short" (Matt. 24:22). We desperately need the Father's help, especially in situations like these. Thus, Jesus teaches us to petition the Father to keep us faithful to him and to preserve us when we are besieged by the evil one. Accordingly, the Lord's Prayer concludes with our asking the Father to help us when the stakes are high and the situation intense: "Do not bring us to the time of trial, but rescue us from the evil one" (6:13).

◼ Conclusion

In the deliverance petition, we ask the Father to keep us faithful to him when we are tempted to disobey him. This may occur in ordinary temptations to sin or in moments of intense, ultimate crisis, wherein we participate to some degree in the eschatological trial. Jesus teaches us that working against us in these situations is Satan, the evil one who seeks our eternal destruction. By enticing and pressuring us to sin, the devil seeks our eternal destruction, which would come by way of our repudiating God in a total (and unrepentant) manner. With this petition, Jesus reminds us of our weakness and our need for the Father's help and protection. He teaches us to petition the Father to preserve us from the full force of the evil one and to keep us faithful to him in times of trial and struggle.

Conclusion

Having come to the end of our study, we can summarize some of its major elements. Like other biblical prayers, the Lord's Prayer contains the words people offer to God. But since this prayer is from Jesus and also part of the Scriptures, the Lord's Prayer is also God's Word to humans. When we say this prayer, not only are we speaking to God, but God is also speaking to us. The Lord's Prayer is a form of divine instruction whereby Jesus teaches us about the Father and about ourselves.

The Lord's Prayer is a prayer to God the Father. Christians can know and address the Father by virtue of our relationship with Jesus, the Father's eternal Son. Through baptism, Christians come to participate in the life of the risen Jesus. Sharing in the life of the risen Jesus, the Son, we also share in his relationship with the Father. Hence, Christians become the Father's adopted children and can address and relate to him as Jesus did. We pray, "Abba! Father!" (Rom. 8:15). This communion with the risen Jesus entails that the baptized are also in a manner of communion with each other: we all share in the one life of the risen Jesus. Accordingly, the Lord's Prayer is a prayer of the community of Jesus's disciples, the church. We are all brothers and sisters in Christ and have the same Father. Hence, we address him as "our Father" (Matt. 6:9). It is through this prayer, moreover, that Jesus invites us to know the Father's goodness and imitate his ways.

The first petition of the Lord's Prayer is the name petition. This petition recalls several Old Testament texts that speak of God's definitive end-time saving act whereby he will manifest his holiness (i.e., sanctify his name). The name petition thus asks the Father to manifest his holiness by bringing his saving plan to its full completion. While God's definitive end-time saving act has already occurred in the death and resurrection of Jesus, Christians look forward to that moment when what has been accomplished in Christ will be fully revealed and realized: the parousia. At that moment, the glory of God will be fully revealed, and people will praise and honor him. The Father will sanctify his name, and then people will sanctify his name.

Much of the same applies to the kingdom and will petitions. The kingdom petition recalls God's promises in Scripture regarding the end-time action of God as king and the state of affairs that results from it. Here too, the definitive end-time saving act of God as king, Christians believe, has occurred in Jesus's death and resurrection. Like the name petition, the kingdom petition looks forward to the parousia, when the Father will fully reveal his kingly rule in Christ and transform the world under his sovereignty. Accompanying this divine action at the parousia is what Matthew specifies in the will petition. When the Father's kingly rule is fully realized in the world, then his sovereign will is going to be done on earth as it is in heaven—perfectly. When the Father's will is done perfectly on earth as in heaven, there will be no place for evil, sin, corruption, and injustice anymore. As we await this action at the parousia, we pray that the Father's kingly will may be done in our own lives. It is a prayer for the faithfulness and obedience of Jesus to become our faithfulness and obedience as the Father's adopted children.

With the bread petition, we ask the Father to provide us with the sustenance we need to live in a manner pleasing to him, both for the present life and for eternity. The Father knows all our needs and gives good things generously. Jesus invites us to "strive first for the kingdom of God and his righteousness" (Matt. 6:33) and have confidence that the Father will provide what we need to live in a manner pleasing to him. This petition also contains an implicit exhortation to be generous and so become the means by which the Father may provide sustenance to others. The bread petition also asks the Father to provide us with the sustenance we need to live with him eternally. This is the food of his heavenly kingdom, the bread of the eschatological banquet. In his ministry and in the life of the church, Jesus makes this eschatological food available to people beforehand, especially in the Eucharist.

With the forgiveness petition, we repent of our sins, acknowledging that we have offended the Father and damaged our relationship with him by our actions. As in the parable of the prodigal son, we should have confidence in the Father's goodness and compassion. For there are no offenses too great or too many that the Father will not readily forgive those who repent. The Father's ways are love, compassion, and forgiveness, and he seeks to form us to be similarly loving, compassionate, and forgiving. Hence, we ask the Father to forgive us in light of our forgiving those who have wronged us. Jesus teaches us that forgiveness and compassion must be a part of the lives of his followers, because forgiveness and compassion are the ways of the Father. By instructing us to pray the forgiveness petition, Jesus both exhorts us and cautions us, for, as he teaches, "The measure you give will be the measure you get" (Matt. 7:2).

The final petitions of the Lord's Prayer are prayers for deliverance. These petitions reveal to us the spiritual battle that is the Christian life in the world. We ask the Father to keep us faithful to him in times of temptation. This may be ordinary temptations to sin or times of intense, ultimate trial when we are tempted to renounce the Father and his Son. In both cases, we ask the Father to help us remain faithfully obedient to him and to protect us from the attacks of the devil.

The Lord's Prayer connects theologically with so many elements in Christian faith: the Trinity; the divine economy, including the course of God's revelation in the history of Israel; the incarnation; the life, death, and resurrection of Jesus; the Holy Spirit; the church and its sacraments; the Christian moral life; prayer, praise, and worship; the parousia; and the eschatological destiny of the people of God. Indeed, one might start to ponder anew the observation of Tertullian that the Lord's Prayer contains, as it were, "a summary of the whole Gospel."[1]

1. Tertullian, *Or.* 1, quoted in Stewart-Sykes, *Tertullian, Cyprian, and Origen*, 42.

Bibliography

Allison, Dale C. *Constructing Jesus: Memory, Imagination, and History.* Grand Rapids: Baker Academic, 2010.

———. *The End of the Ages Has Come: An Early Interpretation of the Passion and Resurrection of Jesus.* Philadelphia: Fortress, 1985.

Anderson, Alistair Scott. "The Imperial Army." In vol. 1 of *The Roman World*, edited by John Wacher, 89–106. London and New York: Routledge, 2002.

Anderson, Gary A. *Sin: A History.* New Haven: Yale University Press, 2009.

Aquinas, Thomas. *The Power of God.* Translated by Richard J. Regan. New York and Oxford: Oxford University Press, 2012.

———. *Quaestiones disputate de potentia.* Translated by Roberto Busa. Textum Taurini 1953 editum. Fundación Tomás de Aquino, 2019. https://www.corpusthomisticum.org/qdp1.html.

Augustine. *The City of God: De Civitate Dei.* Translated by William Babcock. Abridged Study Edition. Hyde Park, NY: New City, 2018.

———. *Commentary on the Lord's Sermon on the Mount with Seventeen Related Sermons.* Translated by Denis J. Kavanagh. Fathers of the Church 11. New York: Fathers of the Church, 1951.

———. *Confessions.* Translated by Henry Chadwick. New York: Oxford University Press, 1991.

———. *Essential Sermons.* Translated by Edmund Hill. Hyde Park, NY: New City, 2007.

Aune, David E. "Prayer in the Greco-Roman World." In *Into God's Presence: Prayer in the New Testament*, edited by Richard N. Longenecker, 23–42. Grand Rapids: Eerdmans, 2001.

———. *Revelation 1–5*. Word Biblical Commentary 52A. Dallas: Word, 1997.

Babylonian Talmud: Seder Zera'im. Berakoth. Edited and translated by I. Epstein and Maurice Simon. London: Soncino, 1948.

Bailey, Kenneth E. *The Cross and the Prodigal: The 15th Chapter of Luke Seen through the Eyes of Middle Eastern Peasants*. St. Louis: Concordia, 1973.

Barr, James. "'Abbā Isn't 'Daddy.'" *Journal of Theological Studies* 39 (1988): 28–47.

Bauckham, Richard. *Jesus and the God of Israel: God Crucified and Other Studies on the New Testament's Christology of Divine Identity*. Grand Rapids: Eerdmans, 2008.

Béchard, Dean P. *Syntax of New Testament Greek: A Student's Manual*. Subsidia Biblica 49. Roma: Gregorian & Biblical Press, 2018.

Betz, Hans Dieter. *Galatians*. Hermeneia. Philadelphia: Fortress, 1979.

———. *The Sermon on the Mount*. Hermeneia. Minneapolis: Fortress, 1995.

Black, C. Clifton. *The Lord's Prayer*. Louisville: Westminster John Knox, 2018.

Blass, Friedrich, Albert Debrunner, and Robert W. Funk. *A Greek Grammar of the New Testament and Other Early Christian Literature*. Chicago: University of Chicago Press, 1961.

Blenkinsopp, Joseph. *Isaiah 1–39*. Anchor Bible 19. New York: Doubleday, 2000.

———. *Isaiah 40–55*. Anchor Bible 19A. New York: Doubleday, 2002.

Bonino, Serge-Thomas. *Angels and Demons: A Catholic Introduction*. Translated by Michael J. Miller. Washington, DC: Catholic University of America Press, 2016.

Bovon, François. *Luke 2: A Commentary on the Gospel of Luke 9:51–19:27*. Translated by Donald S. Deer. Hermeneia. Minneapolis: Fortress, 2013.

Brown, Raymond E. *The Birth of the Messiah: A Commentary on the Infancy Narratives in the Gospels of Matthew and Luke*. New updated ed. Anchor Bible Reference Library. New York: Doubleday, 1993.

———. *The Death of the Messiah*. 2 vols. Anchor Bible Reference Library. New York: Doubleday, 1994.

————. *An Introduction to New Testament Christology.* Mahwah, NJ: Paulist Press, 1994.

————. "The Pater Noster as an Eschatological Prayer." In *New Testament Essays*, 217–53. Milwaukee: Bruce, 1965.

————. *Responses to 101 Questions on the Bible.* New York: Paulist Press, 1990.

Charlesworth, James H., ed. *The Old Testament Pseudepigrapha.* 2 vols. Anchor Bible Reference Library. New York: Doubleday, 1983, 1985.

Clarke, W. Norris. *The One and the Many: A Contemporary Thomistic Metaphysics.* Notre Dame, IN: University of Notre Dame Press, 2001.

Clifford, Richard J. *Creation Accounts in the Ancient Near East and in the Bible.* Catholic Biblical Quarterly Monograph Series 26. Washington, DC: Catholic Biblical Association of America, 1994.

————. *Psalms 1–72.* Abingdon Old Testament Commentaries. Nashville: Abingdon, 2002.

————. *Psalms 73–150.* Abingdon Old Testament Commentaries. Nashville: Abingdon, 2003.

Collins, John J. *The Apocalyptic Imagination: An Introduction to Jewish Apocalyptic Literature.* 2nd ed. Grand Rapids: Eerdmans, 1998.

Davies, W. D., and Dale C. Allison Jr. *The Gospel according to Saint Matthew.* 3 vols. The International Critical Commentary. Edinburgh: T&T Clark, 1988–97.

de la Potterie, Ignace. "The Multiplication of the Loaves in the Life of Jesus." *Communio* 16 (1989): 499–516.

————. "Sin Is Iniquity (1 Jn 3, 4)." In *The Christian Lives by the Spirit*, edited by Ignace de la Potterie and Stanislaus Lyonnet, 37–55. Translated by John Moriss. Staten Island, NY: Alba House, 1971.

Denzinger, Heinrich. *Compendium of Creeds, Definitions, and Declarations on Matters of Faith and Morals.* 43rd ed. Edited by Peter Hünermann, Robert Fastiggi, and Anne Englund Nash. San Francisco: Ignatius, 2012.

de Vaux, Roland. *Ancient Israel.* 2 vols. New York: McGraw Hill, 1965.

DiNoia, J. A. "Knowing and Naming the Triune God: The Grammar of Trinitarian Confession." In *Speaking the Christian God: The Holy Trinity and the Challenge of Feminism*, edited by Alvin F. Kimel Jr., 162–87. Grand Rapids: Eerdmans; Leominster: Gracewing, 1992.

Dodd, C. H. "A Hidden Parable in the Fourth Gospel." In *More New Testament Studies*, 30–40. Grand Rapids: Eerdmans, 1968.

Eichrodt, Walther. *Theology of the Old Testament.* Translated by J. A. Baker. 2 vols. Old Testament Library. Philadelphia: Westminster, 1967.

Emery, Gilles. *The Trinitarian Theology of St. Thomas Aquinas.* Translated by Francesca Aran Murphy. New York: Oxford, 2007.

Eubank, Nathan. "Prison, Penance or Purgatory: The Interpretation of Matthew 5.25–6 and Parallels." *New Testament Studies* 64 (2018): 162–77.

————. *Wages of Cross-Bearing and Debt of Sin: The Economy of Heaven in Matthew's Gospel.* Beihefte zur Zeitschrift für die neutestamentliche Wissenschaft 196. Berlin: de Gruyter, 2013.

Farkasfalvy, Denis. *A Theology of the Christian Bible: Revelation—Inspiration—Canon.* Washington, DC: Catholic University of America Press, 2018.

Fishbane, Michael. *Biblical Text and Texture: A Literary Reading of Selected Texts.* Oxford, UK: Oneworld, 1998.

Fitzmyer, Joseph A. "*Abba* and Jesus' Relation to God." In *À Cause de L'Évangile: Études sur les Synoptiques et les Acts: Mélanges Offerts à Dom Jacques Dupont,* 15–38. Paris: Cerf, 1985.

————. *The Gospel according to Luke.* 2 vols. Anchor Bible. New York: Doubleday, 1970, 1985.

García Martínez, Florentino, and Eibert J. C. Tigchelaar, eds. *The Dead Sea Scrolls: Study Edition.* 2 vols. Leiden: Brill; Grand Rapids: Eerdmans, 2000.

Gerhardsson, Birger. *Memory and Manuscript: Oral Tradition and Written Transmission in Rabbinic Judaism and Early Christianity with Tradition and Transmission in Early Christianity.* Grand Rapids: Eerdmans, 1998.

Green, Joel B. *The Gospel of Luke.* New International Commentary on the New Testament. Grand Rapids: Eerdmans, 1997.

Harrington, Daniel J. *The Gospel of Matthew.* Sacra Pagina. Collegeville, MN: Liturgical Press, 1991.

Heinemann, Joseph, and Jakob J. Petuchowski, eds. and trans. *Literature of the Synagogue.* New York: Behrman House, 1975.

Hemer, Colin J. *The Letters to the Seven Churches of Asia in Their Local Setting.* Grand Rapids: Eerdmans; Livonia, MI: Dove Booksellers, 2001.

Hillers, Delbert R. *Covenant: The History of a Biblical Idea.* Baltimore: Johns Hopkins University Press, 1969.

Holladay, Carl R. *A Critical Introduction to the New Testament: Interpreting the Message and Meaning of Jesus Christ.* 2 vols. Nashville: Abingdon, 2005.

Holmes, Michael W., ed. and trans. *The Apostolic Fathers: Greek Texts and English Translations*. 3rd ed. Grand Rapids: Baker Academic, 2007.

Huizenga, Leroy A. *Loosing the Lion: Proclaiming the Gospel of Mark*. Steubenville, OH: Emmaus Road, 2017.

Jeremias, Joachim. *The Eucharistic Words of Jesus*. Translated by Norman Perrin. Philadelphia: Fortress, 1977.

———. *New Testament Theology: The Proclamation of Jesus*. Translated by John Bowden. New York: Scribner's Sons, 1971.

———. *The Parables of Jesus*. Translated by S. H. Hooke. Rev. ed. London: SCM, 1963.

———. *The Prayers of Jesus*. Translated by John Bowden, Christoph Burchard, and John Reumann. Philadelphia: Fortress, 1967.

Jerome. *Commentary on Matthew*. Translated by Thomas P. Scheck. Fathers of the Church 117. Washington, DC: Catholic University of America Press, 2014.

———. *The Homilies of Saint Jerome*. Vol. 2, *Homilies 60–96*, translated by Marie Liguori Ewald. Fathers of the Church 57. Washington, DC: Catholic University of America Press, 1966.

Johnson, Luke Timothy. *The Writings of the New Testament*. 3rd ed. Minneapolis: Fortress, 2010.

Keener, Craig S. *The Historical Jesus of the Gospels*. Grand Rapids: Eerdmans, 2009.

Kingsbury, Jack Dean. *Matthew as Story*. 2nd ed. Philadelphia: Fortress, 1988.

Klawans, Jonathan. *Purity, Sacrifice, and the Temple: Symbolism and Supersessionism in the Study of Ancient Judaism*. New York: Oxford University Press, 2006.

Kohler, Kaufman. "Ahabah Rabbah ([אהבה רבה], 'Great Love') and Ahabat 'Olam ([אהבת עולם], 'Everlasting Love')." In *The Jewish Encyclopedia*. JewishEncyclopedia.com, 2002–21. https://jewishencyclopedia.com/articles/ 957-ahabah-rabbah.

Kugel, James L. *The Bible as It Was*. Cambridge, MA: Belknap, 1997.

Levenson, Jon D. *The Love of God: Divine Gift, Human Gratitude, and Mutual Faithfulness in Judaism*. Princeton: Princeton University Press, 2016.

Luz, Ulrich. *Matthew 1–7: A Commentary*. Translated by Wilhelm C. Linss. Hermeneia. Minneapolis: Augsburg Fortress, 1989.

———. *Matthew 8–20: A Commentary*. Translated by James E. Crouch. Hermeneia. Minneapolis: Augsburg Fortress, 2001.

————. *Matthew 21–28: A Commentary*. Translated by James E. Crouch. Hermeneia. Minneapolis: Augsburg Fortress, 2005.

Lyonnet, Stanislas, and Léopold Sabourin. *Sin, Redemption, and Sacrifice: A Biblical and Patristic Study*. Analecta Biblica 48. Rome: Biblical Institute, 1970.

MacIntyre, Alasdair. *Dependent Rational Animals: Why Human Beings Need the Virtues*. Chicago: Open Court, 2001.

Malherbe, Abraham J. *Moral Exhortation: A Greco-Roman Sourcebook*. Philadelphia: Westminster, 1986.

Marshall, Bruce D. "Absorbing the World: Christianity and the Universe of Truths." In *Theology and Dialogue: Essays in Conversation with George Lindbeck*, edited by Bruce D. Marshall, 69–102. Notre Dame, IN: University of Notre Dame Press, 1990.

Martin, Francis. "Election, Covenant, and Law." *Nova et Vetera* 4 (2006): 857–90.

————. *The Feminist Question: Feminist Theology in the Light of Christian Tradition*. Grand Rapids: Eerdmans, 1994.

————. *The Fire in the Cloud: Lenten Meditations*. Ann Arbor, MI: Servant, 2001.

————. *The Life-Changer: How You Can Experience Freedom, Power, and Refreshment in the Holy Spirit*. Ann Arbor, MI: Servant, 1990.

Martin, Francis, and Theo Rush. *When You Pray*. Gaithersburg, MD: Word Among Us, 1988.

Martin, Francis, and William M. Wright IV. *The Gospel of John*. Catholic Commentary on Sacred Scripture. Grand Rapids: Baker Academic, 2015.

McCann, J. Clinton, Jr. *The Book of Psalms*. The New Interpreter's Bible 4. Nashville: Abingdon, 1996.

Meier, John P. *A Marginal Jew: Rethinking the Historical Jesus*. 5 vols. Anchor Bible Reference Library. New York: Doubleday, 1991–2016.

Mintz, Alan. "Prayer and the Prayerbook." In *Back to the Sources: Reading the Classic Jewish Texts*, edited by Barry Holtz, 403–29. New York: Touchstone Simon & Schuster, 1984.

Moran, William L. "The Ancient Near Eastern Background of the Love of God in Deuteronomy." *Catholic Biblical Quarterly* 25 (1963): 77–87.

Moore, George Foot. *Judaism in the First Centuries of the Christian Era: The Age of the Tannaim*. 2 vols. New York: Schocken Books, 1971.

Nelson, Richard D. *Raising Up a Faithful Priest: Community and Priesthood in Biblical Theology*. Louisville: Westminster John Knox, 1993.

Nickelsburg, George W. E. "Eschatology (Early Jewish)." In *The Anchor Bible Dictionary*, edited by David Noel Freedman, Gary A. Herion, David F. Graf, and John David Plains, 2:579–94. New York: Doubleday, 1992.

Pennington, Jonathan T. *Heaven and Earth in the Gospel of Matthew*. Grand Rapids: Baker Academic, 2009.

Perrin, Norman. *The Kingdom of God in the Teaching of Jesus*. Philadelphia: Westminster, 1963.

Petersen, David L. "Eschatology." In *The Anchor Bible Dictionary*, edited by David Noel Freedman, Gary A. Herion, David F. Graf, and John David Plains, 2:575–79. New York: Doubleday, 1992.

Pitre, Brant. *Jesus and the Last Supper*. Grand Rapids: Eerdmans, 2015.

———. *Jesus, the Tribulation, and the End of the Exile: Restoration Eschatology and the Origin of the Atonement*. Tübingen: Mohr Siebeck; Grand Rapids: Baker Academic, 2005.

Ratzinger, Joseph. *Jesus of Nazareth Part Two: Holy Week—From the Entrance into Jerusalem to the Resurrection*. Translated by Philip J. Whitmore. San Francisco: Ignatius, 2011.

Rowe, C. Kavin. *Early Narrative Christology: The Lord in the Gospel of Luke*. Grand Rapids: Baker Academic, 2009.

Rowland, Christopher. *The Open Heaven: A Study of Apocalyptic in Judaism and Early Christianity*. New York: Crossroad, 1982.

Roza, Devin. "Pope Francis and the Our Father: Why Context Is Key." *Verbum* (blog), December 28, 2017. https://blog.verbum.com/2017/12/pope-francis-and-the-our-father-why-context-is-key/.

Sakenfeld, Katharine Doob. "Love (Old Testament)." In *The Anchor Bible Dictionary*, edited by David Noel Freedman, Gary A. Herion, David F. Graf, and John David Plains, 4:374–81. New York: Doubleday, 1992.

Sanders, E. P. *The Historical Figure of Jesus*. New York: Penguin, 1993.

———. *Judaism: Practice and Belief; 63 BCE–66 CE*. London: SCM; Philadelphia: Trinity Press International, 1992.

Schiffman, Lawrence H. *Reclaiming the Dead Sea Scrolls: The History of Judaism, the Background of Christianity, the Lost Library of Qumran*. Anchor Bible Reference Library. New York: Doubleday, 1994.

Schlier, Heinrich. *Principalities and Powers in the New Testament*. Quaestiones Disputatae. New York: Herder and Herder, 1961.

Schweitzer, Albert. *The Quest for the Historical Jesus: A Critical Study of Its Progress from Reimarus to Wrede.* Baltimore: Johns Hopkins University Press, 1998.

Second Vatican Council. *Gaudium et Spes.* December 7, 1965. https://www.vatican.va/archive/hist_councils/ii_vatican_council/documents/vat-ii_const_19651207_gaudium-et-spes_en.html.

Seitz, Christopher. "Prayer in the Old Testament or Hebrew Bible." In *Into God's Presence: Prayer in the New Testament,* edited by Richard N. Longenecker, 3–22. Grand Rapids: Eerdmans, 2001.

Smith, Dennis E. "Messianic Banquet." In *The Anchor Bible Dictionary,* edited by David Noel Freedman, Gary A. Herion, David F. Graf, and John David Plains, 4:788–91. New York: Doubleday, 1992.

Sokolowski, Robert. *Eucharistic Presence: A Study in the Theology of Disclosure.* Washington, DC: Catholic University of America Press, 1994.

———. *The God of Faith and Reason: Foundations of Christian Theology.* Notre Dame, IN: University of Notre Dame Press, 1982.

———. *Introduction to Phenomenology.* Cambridge: Cambridge University Press, 2000.

Stegman, Thomas D. "Reading Luke 12:13–34 as an Elaboration of a Chreia: How Hermogenes of Tarsus Sheds Light on Luke's Gospel." *Novum Testamentum* 49 (2007): 328–52.

Stewart-Sykes, Alistair, trans. *Tertullian, Cyprian, and Origen on the Lord's Prayer.* Crestwood, NY: St. Vladimir's Seminary Press, 2004.

Strack, Hermann Leberecht, and Paul Billerbeck. *Das Evangelium nach Matthäus aus Talmud und Midrasch.* 6 vols. Munich: Beck, 1922–61.

Tucker, Gene M. *The Book of Isaiah 1–39.* The New Interpreter's Bible 6. Nashville: Abingdon, 2001.

von Rad, Gerhard. *Studies in Deuteronomy.* Translated by David Stalker. London: SCM, 1953.

Watson, Duane F. "Tribulation." In *Eerdmans Dictionary of the Bible,* edited by David Noel Freedman, Allen C. Myers, and Astrid B. Beck, 1335. Grand Rapids: Eerdmans, 2000.

White, Thomas Joseph. *The Trinity: On the Nature and Mystery of the One God.* Washington, DC: Catholic University of America Press, 2022.

Wright, N. T. *Jesus and the Victory of God.* Minneapolis: Fortress, 1996.

————. "The Lord's Prayer as a Paradigm of Christian Prayer." In *Into God's Presence: Prayer in the New Testament*, edited by Richard N. Longenecker, 132–54. Grand Rapids: Eerdmans, 2001.

————. *The New Testament and the People of God*. Minneapolis: Fortress, 1992.

Wright, William M., IV. *The Bible and Catholic Ressourcement: Essays on Scripture and Theology*. Steubenville, OH: Emmaus Academic, 2019.

Wright, William M., IV, and Francis Martin. *Encountering the Living God in Scripture: Theological and Philosophical Principles for Interpretation*. Grand Rapids: Baker Academic, 2019.

Zimmerli, Walther. *Ezekiel 2: A Commentary on the Book of the Prophet Ezekiel, Chapters 25–48*. Edited by Paul D. Hanson and Leonard Jay Greenspoon. Translated by James D. Martin. Hermeneia. Philadelphia: Fortress, 1983.

Scripture Index

Subject Index

'abbā', 6, 54–55, 63–64, 66, 167
adoption, by Father God, 6, 62–69, 108–10, 160, 167–68
Ahaba Rabbah, the, 46, 88
Amidah, the, 19, 34–35, 45–46
Anderson, Gary A., 132
angels, 31, 47n23, 49, 53–54, 57n43, 75, 85, 90, 103–4, 107, 109, 121–22, 156n23, 157
apocalypticism, 31–32, 53, 92, 99, 105, 122, 162. *See also* eschatology; prophetic restoration
Augustine, 29, 68, 147
Aune, David E., 19

Bailey, Kenneth, 136, 139
baptism
    of Christians, 55, 63, 66–67, 69, 74, 109, 167
    of Jesus, 22, 50, 153
Barr, James, 55
Beatitudes, the, 59, 98, 141
Black, C. Clifton, 68
Brown, Raymond E., 114

child(ren) of God
    Christians as, 6, 62–69, 108–10, 160, 167–68
    Israel as, 39–40, 43–46, 55, 81–82, 117, 135

Jesus's disciples as, 3, 6, 21, 29–30, 57–69, 107–10, 128, 140, 148, 160, 167–68
church, 3, 5, 10n2, 15–16, 27, 29, 38, 51, 66–69, 96, 100, 107, 122, 128, 142, 161, 164–65, 167
covenant. *See* Israel: God's covenant with

Davies, W. D. and Dale C. Allison, 119
devil. *See* Satan
Didache, the, 4, 10n2, 16–17, 19n12
divine pedagogy, 2, 3, 6–7, 9, 26, 28, 36, 45–46, 82
Dodd, C. H., 42

election. *See* Israel: election of
epiousios, 11, 17, 111–14, 121
eschatology, 6, 10, 30–32, 36, 84. *See also* apocalypticism; prophetic restoration
Eubank, Nathan, 145–46
Eucharist, 126–29, 169
evil one. *See* Satan

Father, God as
    of the Davidic King, 40, 44, 47, 49, 65
    of Jesus, 1, 3, 6, 7, 21–22, 24, 29, 37–38, 47–57, 59–69, 74, 87, 101, 106, 108–10, 144, 155, 158–60, 167, 169
    of Jesus's disciples, 6–7, 10–13, 16–24, 29–30, 33–35, 37–38, 47, 56–69,